OF INDIAN CARPETS AND CARPETWALLAHS

Of Indian Carpets and Carpetwallahs
An Appreciation

JON WESTBORG

ALEPH BOOK COMPANY
An independent publishing firm
promoted by *Rupa Publications India*

First published in India in 2023
by Aleph Book Company
7/16 Ansari Road, Daryaganj
New Delhi 110 002

Copyright © Jon Westborg 2023
Carpet photographs: Stian Gulliksrud

All rights reserved.

The author has asserted his moral rights.

The views and opinions expressed in this book are
those of the author and the facts are as reported by him,
which have been verified to the extent possible, and the
publisher is not in any way liable for the same.

No part of this publication may be reproduced,
transmitted, or stored in a retrieval system, in any form
or by any means, without permission in writing from
Aleph Book Company.

ISBN: 978-93-95853-49-1

Printed in India.

This book is sold subject to the condition that it shall
not, by way of trade or otherwise, be lent, resold, hired
out, or otherwise circulated without the publisher's prior
consent in any form of binding or cover other than that
in which it is published.

This book is for very good reasons dedicated to my wife, Trine. For love, companionship, valuable advice, and support through fifty-five years, and postings on three continents. My life would not have been what it was without her. Also, for enduring my hobby, and the time spent on this book—even when she occasionally had difficulties in sharing my fascination with some of the carpets selected.

~

Contents

1. Fascination with Carpets 08
2. Carpetwallahs, Other Traders, and a Bit of Advice 21
3. About Indian Carpets 30
4. About Kashmir and Its Carpet Production 50
5. Carpets from the Deccan and the South 84
6. About Jail Carpets 114
7. The Unappreciated Dhurrie 153

1
Fascination with Indian Carpets

I believe my interest in carpets was kindled by early childhood experiences in India, as exemplified by the first couple of carpets depicted in the following pages. When as a grown-up I returned to the Indian subcontinent, it gave my interest in carpets new opportunities for development. It was, however, not until my posting to New Delhi in the early 1990s that an opportunity presented itself to pursue this fascination seriously, and as somewhat of a passion. In the course of this development, I recognized that carpets certainly could be appreciated for their design, colours, and their 'feel'—even if one does not have any in-depth knowledge of design, material, dyeing techniques or history. A bit of knowledge, however, tends to increase the pleasure.

I also discovered that people generally are pleased by the interest one shows in their carpets, and are more than happy to talk on the subject. More often than not, they parted with information about the origins, how they acquired their carpets, and not the least share the stories that might be associated with them. It gradually dawned on me that apart from their function as decorative elements in their homes, and at times also their monetary value, it was precisely their role as depositories of happy memories or stories that represented their true value. This provided my interest with an additional dimension.

In the beginning, my interest was general in nature. Because of early experience it tilted towards the tribal designs and productions from the Central Asian region. Looking more closely into the subject, I soon understood that in order to build even a rudimentary understanding I needed to concentrate. Viewing the opportunities between the abundance of possibilities of hands-on experiences that Indian carpets provided, and the more limited opportunities that carpets from Central Asian represented, the choice landed on the Indian side. A decision I have never regretted.

In my own purchases, the investment issue has not been central, even if I naturally love to secure good bargains. Initially finding items to enrich our own living environment was the most important consideration. Later interesting designs and representation of carpets from particular areas of India have been guiding my acquisitions. This has provided me with a few admirable pieces, and plenty of good conversations and interesting reading.

In spite of having spent a considerable number of hours on this passion, I am far from able to claim an expertise. I am still only an appreciator. This is also the main reason why I decided to write this book—to share some of my own thrills and experiences associated with this traditional and fantastic example of decorative art from the subcontinent.

A second reason has been that I, in my literature search, found that much of popular literature on carpets pay little attention to productions from India. Moreover, when touching the subject often treat these products as inferior copies of products from other carpet producing regions. I sincerely hope that this book will disprove such views. Further that it might encourage more research—not the least among students in my country of birth.

THE VERY FIRST CARPET

Tibetan medallion carpet

Place of production: Likely Tsang Province, Tibet
Year of production: Probably 1935–1940
Size: 130 cm x 80 cm (4'3"x 2'7")
Material: Wool pile on wool warp and weft
Knot: Firm Tibetan knots
Dye: Natural dyes

As mentioned earlier the value of a carpet will not only be determined by what you paid, or by its technical and aesthetic qualities, but also in my opinion by the story it carries and the memories it awakens. In introducing the first carpet I laid my eyes upon I therefore beg the readers indulgence in a bit of family history.

Ever since I can remember having reflected on the pros and cons of my birth, I have counted it a blessing to have been born to missionary parents. Given their calling, they had to be adventurous—thereby giving me the opportunity to be raised in Assam, on the border of Bhutan, in the northeastern part of India. A most fascinating of places. By the grace of God, and their experiences they regarded all people as equal, and respected the traditions and culture of the many peoples they lived among—thereby instilling also in me the value of such a broad outlook. While never in real poverty, it could hardly be termed a life in riches. The few possessions of any value they acquired, were cherished.

So, it would also have been with this Tibetan carpet that throughout my childhood lay in my parent's bedroom. The reason for this second-hand purchase from a carpetwallah in Darjeeling or Kalimpong during the hot season of 1944 or 1945 was likely that its Tibetan origin reminded my father of his days in Eastern Tibet. Here he had travelled around on horseback from 1938 to 1940 with the purpose of identifying a place to settle and establish a mission station. This pursuit had to be abandoned when Germany invaded Norway while he was on a visit to Hong Kong to marry my

Tibetan medallion carpet
Probably Tsang Province
From 1935–40
130 x 80 (4'3" x 2"3')

mother—and money stopped coming. My father fortunately found employment with an American mission hospital in Canton. After a period of Japanese internment, the family were exchanged with Japanese prisoners in Lorenzo Mark (Beira), then moving onwards to Northeast India—never to set foot in my father's beloved Tibet again.

As Philip Denwood describes in *The Tibetan Carpet*:

> The carpet is, however, also a very good piece of Tibetan weaving – most probably woven in the Tsang province, between Gyantse and Shigatse in the Nyang River valley in south-central Tibet, easily accessible from Kalimpong. In the nineteen-thirties, this area was regarded as the centre of Tibetan carpet industry, both in quality and quantity. Its size indicates that it was made for sitting or sleeping upon. Tibetan wool was used in warp, weft, and pile. The pile dyed with natural dyes. The pattern is a well-designed example of a Tibetan medallion carpet, commonly known as Gyarum.[1]

After my mother died in 1999, the carpet was discovered in a cupboard quite worn out in many places. Instead of disregarding the piece, my wife, Trine, and I brought it to Delhi. Mr Sayeed Ali with assistance of a Tibetan, and considerable effort, brought it back close to its former glory.

The price for the extensive repair undoubtedly exceeded the commercial value of the carpet, but then again, as mentioned above, it is not only the monetary value that acts as the yardstick of appreciation. It's simple beauty; the memories it carries; and the history attached is in the end more important.

---

[1] Philip Denwood, *The Tibetan Carpet*, Aris and Phillips, 1974, pp. 63–65.

THE SECOND CARPET

An Afghan Turkoman

Place of production: Afghan Turkoman
Year of production: Probably around 1945
Size: 185 cm x 130 cm (6'1"x4'3")
Material: Wool pile on wool warp and weft
Knot: Senneh knots 100/sq. inch
Dye: Natural dyes

Carpets can serve their purpose of beautifying the surroundings in more ways than one. So it was with the second carpet I have an affinity to. As with the former, also this Afghan Turkoman carpet from the boarders of Afghanistan is entangled in a family tale.

Every five years or so, my parents were entitled to home furlough. (A very Anglo-Indian term indeed.) This entailed a considerable amount of planning and packing. A change of abode that started with the Indian Railways from wherever in Assam we at that time lived, and to Calcutta (Kolkata). A trip taking two full days, a night, and a ferry crossing of the great Ganges.

Just imaging the impact such a journey and the city of Calcutta would have on children—coming as we were—straight out of an environment which in many aspects was little different from Kipling's jungle.

From Calcutta the journey normally implied another and much longer train ride across the whole of India to Bombay (Mumbai). A long journey, yes, but in my personal opinion there has never been a more exciting and pleasurable way of travelling than that with the old coaches and steam engines of the Indian Railways across the great and varied continent.

Each of their two, four, six, or eight-bed compartments had their separate toilets and opened straight on to the platform at the station. One could not, without considerable danger, move from one compartment to another while the train was running, thus creating a feeling of being in your own small and safe world while on travel. The feeling of security was further heightened by solid burglar bars on all windows—even if here as elsewhere they time and again proved to be mere illusions for those really wanting access. They did, however, keep the beggars at acceptable bay, while still making it possible to enter into haggling with the vendors on the stations for bargain prices as the train was about to leave. The trick for a good price was to conclude the bargain just before the train was leaving the platform and parting the parties forever. Too early, and you would always feel you could have got a better price, too late and you would be travelling on with a craving for that lovely piece of Indian sweet, or the pair of slippers you really had no use of in any case.

The PNO or Lloyd Triestino Liners provided excellent and adventures transportation over the Indian Ocean, up through the Red Sea and the Suez Canal, with possibilities for visits to the free port in Aden, and to Cairo and the pyramids. Then, through the Mediterranean to Naples and Genoa, or onward to Liverpool. The swimming pools; the jazz; rock and dancing; the captain's dinner ball; all made a singular impression compared to the simplicity of the mission station and boarding school; or the herding of cattle on the big plains.

Two days and one night from Genoa would bring us by rail through large parts of Europe all the way to Oslo—and eleven to twelve months of the foreign, but supposedly familiar life and surroundings of Norway.

Thereafter the entire exciting route would be reversed after—mostly my mother having made a rather tearful departure from relatives and friends from one of the two central railway stations in Oslo.

For the parents the entire experience would likely have been regarded at somewhat more of an ordeal. The responsibility for three or four curious and adventure-seeking youngsters; finding accommodation; setting up and dismantling a home; repacking; and replanning. An even greater anxiety would often stem from the fact that more often than not returning missionaries would find themselves located to a new station, new congregations and new accommodation. The latter was certainly the case on one of our returns.

My parents were assigned to a station that had not left the best of impressions from an earlier posting. Whatever the real reason might have been my mother certainly was not thrilled. She was not generally of the complaining sort, but on repeated occasions from we landed in Bombay she kept venting her particular irritation on 'that ghastly patch' in the concrete floor in the middle of the

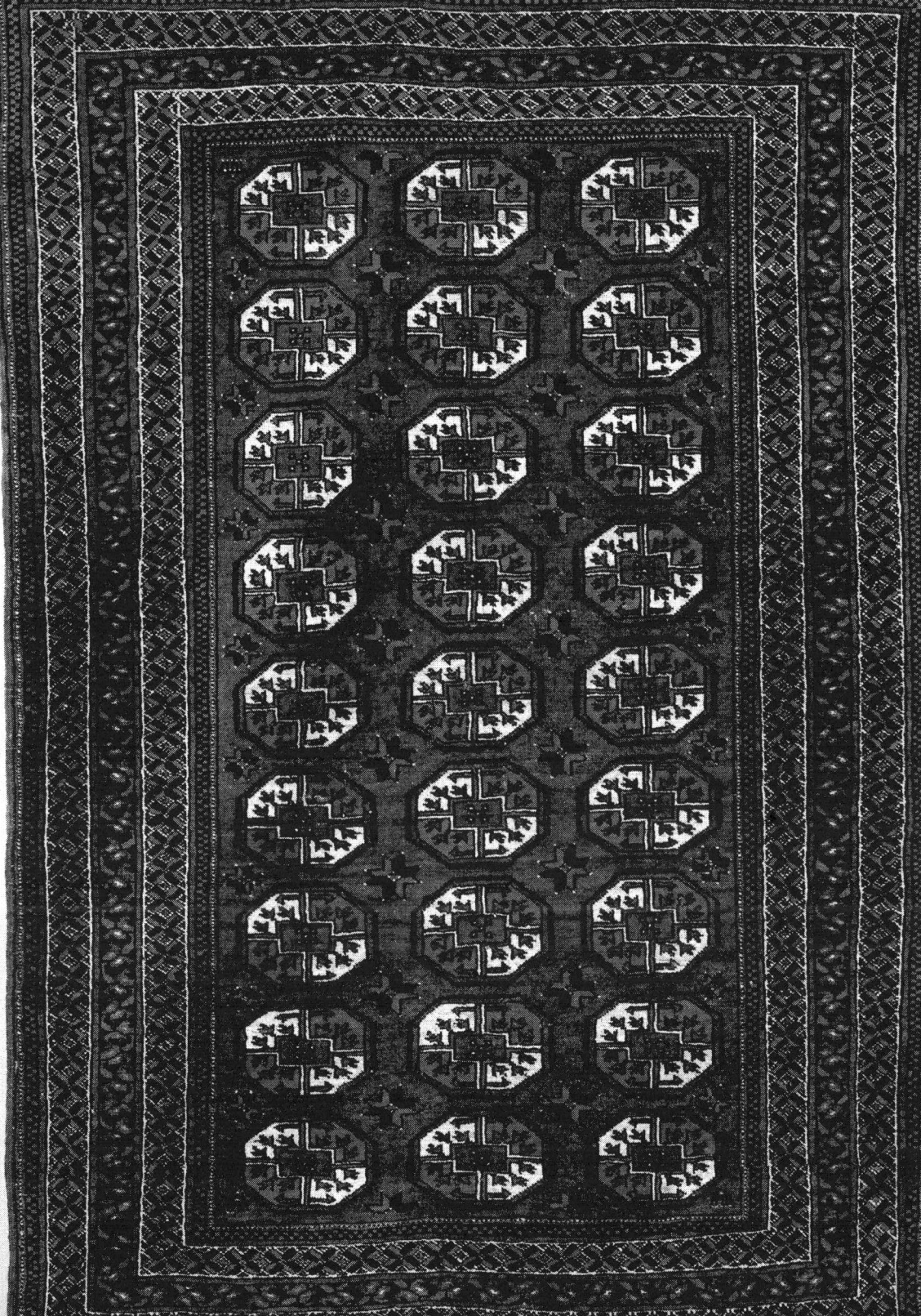

living room in the bungalow. She knew quite well from past experience that nothing could be done without unaffordable expenses.

Her mode—even if she did her best to hide it from her children—did not improve when my father introduced a 4-foot-long cylinder into an already overflowing train compartment. 'Paper for printing of Bible leaflets I got at a very reasonable prize. Can't risk sending them in the luggage compartment,' he claimed quite happily. As my mother later admitted, her nerves were rather in tatters when she stepped into our future living room after the hustle and bustle of the railway station and a dusty Land Rover ride, including a breakdown due to poor maintenance. And there, for all to see was the previously mention ghastly patch in the floor.

Leaving friends and dear ones, the strain of the journey, the anxiety related to the place, and the patch became too much. Tears started flowing until my father in a hurry unwrapped the paper cylinder and rolled out this Turkman carpet, neatly hiding the patch and bringing colour to the stark and barren room. I am certain that it was as much the thought behind my father's purchase as it was the beauty of the carpet that changed the entire atmosphere from gloom to optimism about the future at this arrival.

However, apart from the memories it unearths it is also a beautiful and well-made carpet my father bought second-hand from Shawsons in Calcutta's New Market in 1954. Good wool both in pile, warp and weft, 100 knots/sq. inch, vegetable dyes and a traditional and uncluttered design. By all likelihood it originates from the border areas between Turkmenistan and Afghanistan sometime in the mid-1940s. It may well have been sold to the Shaw family during some of their visits from Kashmir into Afghanistan, but as likely have been brought all the way to Calcutta by one of the many Pathan traders or moneylenders that operated in the eastern part of India prior to and during my childhood. With its subdued and natural dyes and its 6'1"x 4'3" size it fitted nicely into the modest living rooms my parents had, whether in India or Norway. The pile gradually got slightly worn down, but evenly so. Both the fringes and the edges slowly started giving away. It was therefore agreed that I should get it repaired. It greatly benefited from the expert repairs that my carpetwallah, Mr Sayeed Ali, organized and was worth the money.

After my mother's death it gradually came into my hands and will continue to remain in the family, but most likely never again on the floor.

A TURKOMAN INSPIRED KASHMIRI

(*My introduction to Kashmiri Carpets*)

Place of production: Kashmir
Year of production: 1975–80
Size: 183 cm x 122 cm (6' x 4')
Material: Wool on cotton warp and weft;
Knot: Senneh knots, 168/sq. inch woven in Phirayub back
The circumstances and place of purchase

The opportunity to return to the subcontinent of my early years materialized as a consequence of the Bangladesh Liberation War in 1971. More than ten million refugees had crossed into, and been welcomed and taken care of in the state of West Bengal in India. Even with spare rations, ten million more people is a taxing problem for the largest of food reserves, and India of 1972 still had its own occasional famines to deal with. It was therefore paramount that the visitors should return as quickly as possible—a goal the refugees themselves naturally condoned full-heartedly, provided the international community could ensure their survival in independent Bangladesh. Consequently, billions of dollars in emergency and reconstruction assistance streamed into the newly independent Sonar Bangla in the early months of 1972. Accompanying the funds were hundreds, if not a thousand aid workers. Among the latter were also my wife and I, along with our barely two-year old daughter—as one cog in the Lutheran World Service relief and reconstruction machinery.

Rangpur district in the northern part of Bangladesh presented us with two most challenging, taxing, tiring, financially unrewarding, but also emotionally gratifying years of our lives. In order to let off steam and have a change of scenery, we were allowed to leave the war-torn country for more relaxing circumstances a couple of times each year. My wife and I left—of all places—for Calcutta and its New Market.

New Market in Calcutta has from my early childhood been a place of great fascination, intriguing, and a conjurer of imagination. Reading Kipling's description in *Kim* of the market places of Lahore brought in my early years automatically New Market to mind. It is an unbelievable maze of alleys

and back alleys; all covered by continuous series of roofs, with invisible demarcations that separated one type of product from another. Furniture in one area; handicraft in another; tools and hardware separated from both pets and fabrics. And all the way in the back was the submarket for fish and meat—not the most sanitary of butcher or fishmonger's shops.

New Market used to pride itself of being be able to supply you with all your heart desired—from a jar of Marmite to spare-parts for your Rolls-Royce. You might have to wait a couple of weeks for the latter, but arrive it would. A characteristic story from the market goes as follows: A Norwegian missionary was aggressively pacing down one of the alleys while looking into various shops on his way. One of the many touts who would encourage customers to particular shops for a few rupees from grateful shop owners, approached the man with a certain familiarity, and asked him kindly to follow him. With considerable suspicion the man refused. The tout continued imploring him to follow while suggesting various wares he thought might interest the missionary. After having traversed a few crossroads and becoming quite exasperated with the pestering tout the missionary stopped and burst out: 'I am not interested in anything you might suggest, and you would in any case not be able to get me what I want since I am looking for my wife. Upon which the tout—pointing to a shop but few paces down the alley—replied: 'But, sahib, I know she is in there.' Of course, this might originally have been a planter or even a tourist—but nevertheless a describing story and good PR for the market.

OUR VERY FIRST OWN CARPET

Staying at the Lytton Hotel—a modest, but clean establishment close to the market—also we, with good help from service minded coolies, found the food items and other necessities that were not easily available in the war-ravaged country of our residence. Trine and I also found beautiful Kashmiri carved walnut furniture. Furniture that—when we several years later unpacked it in Norway—fitted nicely together, with not a single crack in spite of the dry Norwegian winter weather.

Following in my father's footsteps, we found our way to Shaw Sons—stockist of Persian, Bukhara & Kashmir carpets; manufacturer of embroideries, carpet & shawls, etc.

Here we were treated as royalty, our well-being looked after with cups of good, sweet chai, and taken very seriously in our pursuit of buying our very first carpet. After several cups of tea, and having viewed and discussed fifteen to twenty different carpets, we walked out with a 'Bukhara of Kashmiri design'. When I later came to understand what sums of money these people turned over in their daily trade I could but wonder why, but certainly appreciate, that they bothered to make such effort with a young couple that had so little to spend. But such seems to be the habit and pleasure of good Indian carpet traders when they meet someone with a genuine interest in their art. We have been indebted both for the carpet, and the treatment for forty-five years.

A Turkoman-inspired Kashmiri

There are in my opinion three issues worth mentioning about this pleasing, but unassuming traditional 4'x6' piece of carpet from this period.

Firstly, that it neither is a Tekke, an Afghan, nor a Yomud rug. Neither is it a Bukhara. The city of Bukhara was in fact never a carpet producing centre, but a reputed collection point and market for tribal carpets from considerable areas of Central Asia. Bukhara carried a marketing mystic and lure similar that of Samarkand or Timbuktu. It was therefore—before research really entered into the arena of rugs and carpets—quite common with names such as Teke-Bukhara, Yomud-Bukhara.[2] For a similar reason, carpets such as this was sold as Kashmiri-Bukharas—often conveniently forgetting the Kashmir part of the name—by the less truthful members of the trade. As it will be noted from the enclosed receipt my wife and I was properly informed. It is not a Bukhara, not even a tribal carpet, but a carpet designed and produced at a workshop or home in Kashmir, and was sold and should be judged as such. Since the carpet bears strong resemblance to the some of the Turkman Mauri carpets from Herat, the appropriate way of describing the carpet should probably have been a 'Turkoman-inspired Kashmiri' carpet.[3]

Secondly the colours are pleasing, the wool of good quality and with firm knotting. I must, however, agree with K. Chattopadhyaya that it tends to be somewhat unstable on the floor and behaves better with a good underlay. The reason being that while it, as most Indian carpets, use the Persian knot it does so with a variation. In this Phirayub type of knotting the number of knots of pile in the length of carpet is nearly twice as high as the width—in this case 12/20 with cotton warp and a single strand of wool weft.[4]

Thirdly, and contrary to what has been claimed by some, the manner in which it is knotted does not seem to reduce it longevity. After more than forty years of active use—with three children in the house—it still is in excellent shape and without blemishes.

A worthwhile purchase for a couple who could not afford anything more expensive at that stage in their lives!

---

[2]Nathaniel Harris, *Rugs and Carpets of the Orient*, Hamlyn Publishing Group, 1977.
[3]R. D. Parsons, *Oriental Rugs*, Volume 3, The Carpets of Afghanistan, p.134.
[4]K. Chattopadhyaya, *Origin of Pile Carpets and their Development in India*, Marg XVIII.

2

Carpetwallahs, Other Traders, and a Bit of Advice

THE CARPETWALLAHS OF DELHI

You occasionally see them on the roads and lanes of Delhi—black and yellow taxis or three-wheelers laden to the overflow with carpets, some new, but mostly second-hand Indian, Persian, Chinese, Turkman, or Afghan. On the top of the pile or next to the driver sits an ordinary clothed man (never a woman) of varying age. They are—nearly without exception—members of the carpetwallahs of Delhi. Quite often, but not always, they are Kashmiris.

Among themselves, they recognize some fifteen others operating the trade in Delhi. They have no organization, they are definitely competitors, and do not seem to recognize individual turfs. They do, however, occasionally meet, and do at times trade with each other.

They do not represent a new phenomenon. Their manner of trading is one that has existed parallel with the stands on the old market places, and it still fills a niche in the broader carpet trade. They sell, but they also purchase. They represent an excellent outlet for middle-upper class people who have fallen on hard times and need someone whom with discretion can relieve them of their carpets, through an outright purchase or for a decent commission. Or, for people, who have given their living room a 'makeover' and want to find a matching carpet by discreetly exchanging the one they have, making up the difference in cash—paying or receiving as the case might be. Most of them have a good knowledge of carpets, and a few of them rightfully should be called experts.

They arrive at your doorsteps at a time of your choice, and will leave the carpets you choose for a few days, or even a week if your schedule so require. Leaving you in your own surroundings with plenty of time to ponder the chosen carpet's quality, colours, overall suitability, and price, the carpetwallahs provide an ideal way for a customer to buy a carpet.

Among those I made acquaintance none deserved to be called crooks—they would soon find it difficult to remain in the business if that was the case. This, however, does not mean that some of them would not tell you a far-fetched story, or add some years to the age of an old carpet with the aim to increase your interest and thereby their profit from a transaction. Some of them—like

Carpetwallah Sayeed Ali

horse traders—unquestionably know, and fall to the temptation of using the tricks necessary to make the carpets look their best, or rather better than their best, by doctoring their faults and hiding their weaknesses.

However, they were all great fun, provided interesting conversations, and made it possible to study carpets I otherwise would never have seen. They created an appreciated diversion of mind that otherwise tended to get stuck in work. I am most obliged for the time they spent, the stories they provided, and the knowledge they parted.

From most of them, I actually never bought a carpet since my interest only was in old and antique Indian products. I gradually discovered that such carpets needed special efforts to be found, and the one man that seemed able to oblige with variety and quality was a carpetwallah by the name of Mr Sayeed Ali of Sayeed Carpets.

Mr Sayeed is a soft-spoken Kashmiri, a devoted Muslim of the Sufi tradition. He was born in Kashmir in 1954. His father was according to Sayeed a man with great knowledge of weaving, washing, and repairing carpet, but also a respected trader. They moved to Delhi in 1972 and it was from his father he learned the trade, and introduced to the particulars of carpets from many of the world's carpets centres.

When he first visited my residence in Shanti Niketan in New Delhi in 1991, he peddled more of Persian, Afghan, and other Central Asian carpets than those made in India. In my limited understanding, his wares were slightly more expensive than those supplied by other carpetwallahs, but uniformly of good quality, and he was quick to point out any defects. Understanding that I was primarily interested in old Indian carpets he promised to start looking for such.

He nevertheless asked me to take a closer look at a beautiful approximately 9' x 6' Persian carpet which he insisted would be a worth purchasing, and left it with me for a couple of weeks to make up my mind. The carpet according to Sayeed came from a specific village in the eastern part of Iran—which I unfortunately now do not remember—and would have been made around 1920. I took due note of his claim and since I had to travel to Norway the same week, I decided to take the carpet with me in order to test the information with a well-known Norwegian expert on Persian carpets. Wanting an unbiased opinion, I did not divulge the information I had received from Sayeed. The Norwegian expert's immediate reaction was that this was a carpet of a type not often seen. However, pointing to some of the characteristics of the design and structure, he proceeded to name the same village as Mr Sayeed had mentioned. Further, in his estimation the carpet was produced soon after World War II. Due to its place of origin, the age, and that it was without blemish he would be pleased to sell it on commission for a price thrice I had been quoted by Mr Sayeed. Tempting as it was, I remained steadfast in my resolve to concentrate on Indian carpets. The visit was, however, an excellent confirmation of Mr Sayeed's knowledge of his trade. Also at a later date, I used a similar opportunity to test his abilities, with equally good result.

Mr Sayeed also proved to stand by his promise to find old and antique Indian carpets, and brought such to my house at regular intervals. At this time, I also began seeking carpet literature in books[1] and magazines such as *Haldi* and *Oriental Rug Review*, and in catalogues from auctions at Christie's and Sotheby's. They all indicated a growing interest in antique Indian carpets. Mr Sayeed who is a modest man attributes his ability to find, judge, and procure these old products to the knowledge he gained from his father. This knowledge also included carpets and durries from the jails. Already during his father's time, there had been foreigners who were interested in old Indian carpets in general, and jail carpets and durries in particular. These had sought out his father for advice that otherwise was hard to come by.

The early 1990s was a time when a growing general interest in old Indian arts and craft products surfaced among well-to-do Indian business people. It was also the time of the great turnaround of the Indian economic liberalization. Sitting well placed to observe these changes; I also noticed that prices on antique specimens of several Indian art forms suddenly started skyrocketing. This was not only a result of foreign interest, but definitely also from the well-to-do Indians. My assumption was that also Indian carpets would be 'discovered' and that their value would increase substantially. So, as a manner of gratitude to Mr Sayeed's kindness in looking for old and antique carpets I purchased the carpets I could afford, but also supplied him with such information and analyses. Gradually a relationship beyond mere business developed.

I left my land of birth again in the autumn of 1993, but my work permitted me to make regular

---

[1] David Black, *World Rugs & Carpets*, Country Life Books, 1985; Ian Bennet; Rugs & Carpets of the World, Tiger, reprint 1988; Ian Bennett; Jail Birds: An Exhibition of 19th Century Indian carpets, Kennedy Carpets, 1987.

visits to Delhi over the next decade. Therefore, contact was maintained and carpets were bought both for my small collection as well for acquaintances of mine. During this period, Mr Sayeed started concentrating on old Indian carpets—naturally those produced in Kashmir, but not the least carpets and durries produced in the jails. This meant travelling out of Delhi to places all over India wherever these carpets were found. This increased his knowledge of their variety and availability, and provided a network of both potential sellers and buyers. When the interest for these carpets took off in the mid-1990s he was therefore well placed to trade in Delhi and other commercial centres in India, but also cater to some of the European and American buyers who regularly visit the country.

When I return as ambassador to India in 2003, I was therefore privileged—whether I bought or not—to be given a first look at his findings. This gave me an opportunity to view a quantity of old Indian carpets which, along with the conversation that followed, gradually gave me quantity enough to develop some 'feel' of what production centres they likely originated from.

I remain indebted to Mr Sayeed as a source of both unwritten knowledge and inspiration for further research.

THE OFFICIAL CARPET SHOPS AND A BIT OF ADVICE

I have come to believe that there must be some carpet shops in every city in India, and that in places like Delhi, Mumbai, Kolkata, and Chennai they are numerous. For most customers, they represent the only viable option for carpet purchases. You will find them in the larger hotels, at the markets, and in close proximity to some of the tourist sites. It pays to visit them without a tourist guide or one of the many 'helpers' you are likely to encounter in such places. It is better that you, not they get the benefit of the commission the outlet feels obliged to provide for having introduced you to the premises.

For many—particularly non-residents to a country or a city—entering a carpet shop is a bit of a challenge. There are rightly or wrongly so many stories circulating about people who have got badly 'conned' in these establishments. To purchase your carpet from an outlet near the place you live is therefore not a bad advice. Except, of course, that it takes away, the fun of having a product you yourself have bought in its place of origin. *If this is an important consideration, I am sure you will be able to find a lot of advice in literature or on the web. Whatever you might find, however, do not purchase a cheap carpet in its place of origin just because you believe that you thereby get a fantastic bargain.* Merchants in your home cities are generally in a much better position than you to strike a good deal, particularly on run-of-the-mill products. Many are those who come home only to find that they could have bought the same style and quality at a better price in their own locality.

From my personal experience—whether I have been in a resident or non-resident position—there are four criteria with which one should enter the challenge: at least a couple of hours of time; some knowledge of carpets from the region in question; readiness to walk out if you do not find a carpet you are not absolutely certain fits its purpose; and some pictures depicting the colours in the room where you want to use the carpet.

The latter is self-explanatory, but often forgotten. Time is of essence both for your own frame of mind, as well as for the manner in which you are likely to be treated. One should be careful in judging the salesman too harshly for being pushy since customers—particularly foreigners—either do not bother or simply do not understand that a satisfactory purchase of a carpet cannot be expedited in the same time as buying a shirt. What satisfaction remains in such circumstances for those among the merchants who really want to assist their customers—except an excessive profit? I therefore have great admiration for the merchant who understanding that I came into his shop with very little time to spare plainly suggested that I should leave and come back when I was ready to give the time such a purchase required. I left, but made a point of returning when I visited the same city a few months later.

A bit of knowledge is always useful because it can enable you to ask pertinent questions, and therefore be judged a person of substance. However, do not try to impress the salespersons with your knowledge. Usually, they know much more than you have been able to pick up. Moreover, do not outright argue their information. If the information is of importance, but obviously wrong, it is better to rephrase your question in a manner that shows that you know that the information is incorrect. If the salesperson persists, I believe the best would be to find a feeble excuse for leaving the premises, thereby indicating that you are unhappy. This is far more polite than entering into an argument that leaves both of you irritated or feeling wounded. This approach certainly also applies to the general art of bargaining.

Without a resolve to either find what you are looking for, or leave, you are easily manipulated. Believe my experience when I say that the people you are dealing with are usually experts in reading your frame of mind. Therefore, listen carefully to their arguments because they may have the argument you need. If not, thank them for their time and hospitality, and explain that you are not certain and need time to ponder the decision.

The above approach has worked well for me with the serious merchants. It might also help when encountering the unfortunate many that only want to make a quick sale. They consequently tend to oversell or attempt to overpower their customers with dubious information and stories. They present their price based on their assessment of their customer's pocket or level of knowledge, rather than the quality of their product, or do not bother to take time to listen to their customer's needs. These are also often those that are unable to assist their customers in making choices he or she are pleased with—long years after they place their purchase on the floor of their homes. I have certainly come across some of this category. Their existence is a great pity also for the good traders. It leaves too many interested people with a feeling of uncertainty about their purchase, and end up being poor or even negative ambassadors for these beautiful pieces of Indian decorative arts.

Some might find the above advice a tedious way of doing business, but it has given me many pleasant hours of carpet viewing and conversation in India over many years. Pleasant hours starting from my first encounter with Shaw and Sons at their outlet in Kolkata in the early 1970s, continuing with the same family's outlet in Le Meridien Hotel in New Delhi over the last twenty years, as well as other shop owners such as a surprising encounter in Bombay.

A BOMBAY SURPRISE

Understand Your Customer's Need

Place of production: Kashmir
Year of production: 1975–1980
Size: 275 cm x 185 cm (9' x 6'1")
Material: Wool with white silk inlay, cotton warp and weft
Knot: Senneh knots, 324/sq. inch woven in Jaipur back

Life is full of surprises. In the spring of 1982, our assignment for Save the Children Norway in Sri Lanka was ending. After a rather hectic period, my wife and I decided to take a few days leave and travel to Mumbai with the aim of buying a carpet for our living room in Norway. The whole venture was a spur of the moment decision, no e-mail existed and the telephone network in both Mumbai and Colombo were inadequate to put it mildly. Not to mention the connection between the two cities. The result was that we ended up in Mumbai without a confirmed hotel reservation—in a city that just that week had decided to hold a large medical conference with doctors from all over India and abroad in attendance. The hotel, to which a booking had been forwarded, was ever so helpful and did their best to find alternative accommodation. This, however, naturally took time.

In the meantime, my wife and I start our search in a carpet outlet on the hotel premises. After having explained the reason for our visit and our predicament, and after having looked at various options available, the shop manager concluded that he did not have what we required. However, he did believe he understood what we were looking for. If we would be bothered to return around lunchtime the following day, he would take us to an outlet where he was sure they had what we were looking for. We gratefully agreed.

Fortunately, the hotel managed to secure some decent accommodation in another part of the city. The next day we continued our search while waiting for lunchtime. In a shop close to the Gateway of India, we actually found one we thought fit our needs. For bargaining reasons, however, we avoided showing our interest in any particular carpet. On our arrival at the former shop, the manager

A Turkoman-inspired Kashmiri 1975–80
183 x 122 cm (6'4" x 4')

immediately secured a taxi at his own cost, and off we went. To our complete amusement, it turned out to be the same shop in which we had been that very morning—which we naturally told him. The staff, of course, also informed him of the same, but he said he wanted us to have a look at one particular carpet he knew they had, where after he selected the same carpet we had made up our mind to purchase if he did not turn up something better. We bought their carpet.

It could, of course, have been a coincidence, but my wife and I—after going through the incident—came to the conclusion that the man really knew his job and understood the needs of his customers.

Apart from now being accompanied by an amazing story, the carpet is a very good example of Kashmiri carpets from this period—quite detailed and rich, with appropriate knot count and a strong border. It is excellently crafted, and the use of white silk enhances the details of the individual elements in the field. I have later discovered that quite a number of carpets with this peculiarity seem to have been made in Kashmir in the late 1970s and early 1980s—before complete silk carpets became common in their production. More than thirty years of active service in our living room, and not a blemish. Its traditional design and colour scheme blends well with our old Sri Lankan cupboards and burgomaster chairs. The use of a simple glass top table allows us to see the carpet, even if we follow a Norwegian tradition of keeping a carpet under the dining table.

3
About Indian Carpets

There are indications of 'piled carpet' production existing in the north-western part of the subcontinent prior to the fifteenth century. No conclusive evidence in the form of whole carpets or fragment of carpets have, however, as yet surfaced.

This is not really surprising. The climate in large parts of the Indian subcontinent along with a population settled with agriculture as livelihood—rather than nomadic livestock—made cotton the preferred material, and the tapestry-woven 'durrie' the natural product of choice. These durries were cooler, more hardy, and the material more easily available and affordable than piled carpets. The durries therefore presented a more natural and flexible produce for personal use, cottage production, and common artistic expression. The piled woollen carpets on the other hand were therefore, and have continued to be, products of luxury for the small affluent part of the society in India as well as in the West.[1]

The first documented efforts to introduce production of woollen piled carpets into the subcontinent seem to have followed as a consequence of Timur's rise to power in Central Asia. When Timur in 1398 invaded India, the sultan of Kashmir sent his son, Prince Zain-ul-Abidin to pay homage to Timur. Timur took the prince hostage and kept him for the next seven years. In spite of his reputation for violence Timur was a strong patron of art and ensured by persuasion or force that artists from all over his domain settled and worked in the capital—among these also those engaged in carpet production. Becoming impressed by the arts and crafts of Samarkand during his forced stay, the prince brought with him a number of artisans when he returned to Kashmir. Some of these were carpet weavers. When he later ascended the throne, he also secured carpet craftsmen from Persia and got the industry started in Kashmir.[2]

A better-known initiative was that of Emperor Akbar who around 1580 brought some Persian carpet weavers to India and set up a workshop in his palace in Agra. Later royal factories were established in such cities as Fatehpur, Delhi, and Lahore. This patronage was followed up by his successors Jahangir and Shah Jahan. The surviving carpets from this period exist both in Indian,

---
[1]Tirthankar Roy, *Traditional Industry in the Economy of Colonial India*, 1999.
[2]Jasleen Dhamija, *Marg*, Vol. XVIII September 1965, p. 32.

European, and American museums, and in private collections. They are regarded as some of the best and most interesting carpets ever produced. With royal patronage, the art spread to further areas on the subcontinent.

A less recognized avenue of introduction took place in the south-eastern part of the subcontinent—in Masulipatnam and Elluru in present-day Andhra Pradesh—probably well before Akbar introduced his Persian weaver to the North. No written records are unearthed from that time of this event. However, Sir Streynsham Master refers to this verbal history in his memoirs from 1657. Henry T. Harris also concludes in his discussion of the subject, that there are reasons to assume the industry in this area actually dates from about the middle of the fifteenth century.[3] Finally, Jasleen Dhamija[4] supported this assumption based on interviews with descendants of these families as part of her research in 1965.[5]

It is not, unreasonable to assume that this southern production gradually spread to other areas in the South, such as Warangal, Gulbarga, Hyderabad, and Aiyampet. In the three former it would likely to have come in touch with Akbar's northern introduction.

Daniel Walker in his publication related to the exhibition 'Flowers Underfoot: Indian carpets of the Moghal Era' recognize that the carpet production in the Deccan contributed significantly to production and export of carpets of considerable artistic value from the early part of the seventeenth century onwards. It should also be noted that carpets from this region were influential in creating the revival of interest in subcontinental carpets following the Great World Exhibition of 1851 in London.[6]

From the three initial centres mentioned above, the knowledge and technique in preparation of the basic material, designs, knotting, and finishing of carpets spread out quite rapidly to many places on the subcontinent—greatly assisted by patronization of the Mughal emperors, their local rulers, courts, and vassals.

Initially these carpets naturally were of Persian design. As Indian weavers got trained, and the offspring of Persian weavers grew up on the subcontinent, they gradually introduced elements which gave the carpets a specific Indian flavour in style and realism, and with typical Indian flowers and animals in place of Persian. The Persian influence, however, quite naturally continued over

---

[3]Henry T. Harris, *Carpet Weaving Industry of Southern India*, 1908.
[4]Marg Vol. XVIII, September 1965, p. 32.
[5]The issue is further elaborated on in chapter xxx.
[6]Daniel Walker, *Flowers Underfoot: Indian Carpets of the Mughal Era*, Thames and Hudson, 1998.

the centuries, but Indian carpet-making also influenced production in certain parts of Persia. Such interchange of artistic expressions continues even today.

Oriental carpets had by the end of the sixteenth century become fashionable among the elites in Europe. From the early part of the seventeenth century there are documented evidence of trading companies as well as individuals from England, Holland, Portugal, and probably also smaller European countries, becoming engaged in securing carpets for a growing European market. The first consignment of 'Lahore' carpets—as they were called—left Surat for England in 1615. This resulted in increased number of orders. The British East India Company primarily sought carpets from the workshops in Lahore, but also from those that existed in Agra, Jaunpur (east of Agra), Fatehpur, Ajmer, Cambay, and certainly in Kashmir. For carpets from these areas, they would have competed with Dutch and Portuguese merchants who are known to have engaged in this trade. The Dutch had in addition already from 1666 secured carpets from the Deccan (Eluru, Masulipatnam, Warangal, and Hyderabad) for their home markets, and even for trade with Japan.

The problem merchants faced was scarcity of supply and consequently higher prices. The competition was not only between the European traders, but more so with local dignitaries. Further, the factories tended to produce on direct requests—not to a market. Reports show that European traders experienced this as a time-consuming process. They also discovered that the carpets produced on their orders did not provide the same quality as those they found under production for the rulers or local dignitaries.

In spite of these obstacles, a good number of carpets were shipped to England, Holland, and Portugal during the seventeenth century. Records as late as in 1683 indicate large orders from English and Dutch firms. Many of these carpets are still to be found in museums and in private residences in Europe. At the end of the century, the English trade seems to have tapered off, while the Dutch continued this trade well into the eighteenth century, possibly because they also had cultivated a supply chain in the Deccan.[7]

The scarcity seems to have increased during the eighteenth century. This was not because the skills or talents disappeared. More likely because of the 'industry's' inherent dependency on patronage from the rulers and aristocracy for quality production. This shifted from one place to another and at times back again. And the rise and fall tended to happened in some synchronization with the rise and fall of dynasties, power centres, and their aristocracy. Particularly in the North these local clients seem to

---

[7] Ibid, p. 15.

have been viewed as more stable 'masters' than European merchants—whose culture, religion, taste, or business practices were difficult to fandom by those organizing and producing the carpets.

The above theory is supported by the historian Tirthankar Roy. Based on research he attributes the trend to the decline of power of the Mughal empire. The decline resulted in an attack on Delhi by Nadir Shah in 1731, during which a number of carpet workshops were destroyed. These were workshops patronized by the Indian aristocrats, and probably also European merchants. It also caused a general political decentralization that forced the empire to accept that their local rulers increased their independence.

As the real power of the emperors in Delhi waned, these local rulers needed to demonstrate their wealth and power, and they had the affluence to do so. Carpets and carpet production were among the luxuries that represented such wealth, and so did the ability to afford the establishment of good carpet workshops. Rulers from these areas are therefore documented to have secured craftsmen to their own palace workshops from power centres in decline, or where new rulers with less interest in this art emerged at the old centres. This in turn created environments where the art of carpet-making to develop and prosper at such regional centres as Kashmir, Hyderabad, Bihar, and Mysore.[8]

At the same time a market for 'oriental carpets' also re-emerged in Europe. The European merchant houses trading on India, however, did not initially react by seeking to establish their own workshops or even to attempt to influence the production by demanding changes in design or colouring on any scale.[9]

It is also surprising that the European market was not more actively exploited by the new Indian entrants to the field. This might indicate that the new rulers and other aristocrats viewed their involvement as that of patrons of an art or as a way of securing the requirements for their palaces, rather than as a commercial activity.

This patronage culture did not result in large scale production. Nor did it keep Indian carpet on the radar screen of European connoisseur or carpets dealers. Nevertheless, it undoubtedly kept the art of carpet-making alive and in development through the latter part of the eighteenth and first half of the nineteenth century.[10] The quality of, and praise showered on carpets from India during the Great

---

[8] Tirthankar Roy, *Traditional Industry of the Economy of Colonial India*, p. 200.
[9] There is documentation where 'factories' operated by the East Indian Company or others merchant houses are mentioned. A factory was, however, a common term for the trading and warehouse facilities that such companies operated, rather than a workshop for carpet production.
[10] David Black, *World Rugs & Carpets*, 1985, pp. 194–95.

World Exhibition of 1851 is ample testimony to these assumptions.

(While this late part of eighteenth and beginning of nineteenth century development is surprising from a commercial point of view, it might actually have saved the 'Indian character' of this art through this period from the negative aspects that followed efforts to meet re-emerging demands in the nineteenth century.)

THE GREAT REVIVAL

The results of the Great London Exhibition of 1851 brought about considerable activities to reinvigorate the industry, and most of the areas where there still were some skills and knowledge were reactivated.[11]

While the increased European and American demands resulted in increased production it also created pitfalls. These resulted in decline in quality, and in certain cases outright sloppy products. Some literature from the latter part of nineteenth and early part of the twentieth century have been interpreted as indicating that Indian products generally was devoid of both artistic quality as well as poor workmanship. This, however, was not the case and such interpretation is also a simplification of what was actually written. Since my experiences indicate that these interpretations have had considerable negative impact on the reputation of Indian carpets even today, the issue is worth some deliberation.

Recognized authorities such as Sir George Birdwood, J. K. Mumford and others in the latter part of nineteenth and early part of the twentieth century certainly lamented on the deterioration of all aspects of carpet making on the subcontinent, from the wool and dyeing, to artistic character, and weaving. A closer study, however, reveals that their criticism is primarily founded on study of carpets made for export. They also placed the responsibility for the poor quality squarely on the European traders. In order to cash in on trends in their respective markets and increase volume of sales these traders prescribed poor wool and low knot-counts, but also demanded changes to designs—incorporating European elements into traditional designs, as described in the following.

Birdwood writes in 1884 about the carpets from Masulipatnam that they were formerly among the finest produced in India, but of late years have also been corrupted by the European, chiefly English demand for them. The English importers insisted on supplying the weavers with cheaper materials, and now we find that these carpets are invariably backed with English twine. The spell of tradition

---

[11]Ibid.

thus broken, one innovation after another was introduced into the manufacture. The designs which of old were full of beautiful details, and more varied than now in range of scheme and colouring, were surrounded by a delicate outline suggested as to tint by a harmonising contrast with colours with which it was in contact. But the necessity for cheap and speedily executed carpets for the English market has led to the abandonment of this essential detail in all Indian textile ornamentation. Crude inharmonious masses of unmeaning form now mark the spot where formally varied, interesting and beautiful designs blossomed as delicately as the first flowers of spring: and these once glorious carpets of Masulipatnam have sunk to a mockery and travestie of their former selves.[12]

J. Forbes Watson in a short note two years later writes that in some areas 'the attempt to imitate European patterns is producing a degradation in character of the production which if persisted in, will prove fatal to the trade. In place of the beauty and truthfulness of the native design, some of the carpets and rugs imported into this country are simply hideous ...... Common European chintz patterns intermixed with distorted remains of the fine native designs. These errors are not those into which the native artist will fall, *if left to himself.*'[13]

Birdwood also identified the introduction of carpet making into the jails as a strong contributing factor to the deterioration in the production on the subcontinent, and made it something of a crusade to see this practise stopped. While recognizing the inherent dangers of the practice, and the damage it had done to the 'free' carpet makers other writers of the time argued that the jail production—after the initial face—contributed positively to development of the art in many localities. In other area they had contributed to revival of carpet making where it otherwise would have disappeared altogether.[14]

Writers on the topic, however, generally recognized that parallel with the above decline in many areas there were good and even excellent carpets being produced in other localities. Some of these entered the export market, but more importantly were produced for royalty, aristocrats and other dignitaries—local and foreign—on special orders. Sir George Watt's comprehensive research on the subject for the Indian Art exhibition in Delhi 1902 clearly demonstrates this variety in full.[15] The same does Henry T. Harris in his extensive monograph on the carpet industry in Southern India from 1908.[16]

---

[12] Birdwood p. 381.
[13] Watford p. 142.
[14] See chapter on Jail Carpets.
[15] Sir George Watt; Official Catalogue for Delhi Exhibition, 1903.
[16] Henry T. Harris, *Monograph, Carpet Weaving Industry of Southern India*, Madras, 1903.

CARPET MAKING—A DECORATIVE ART

In the above connection, it is worth remembering that carpets were and are made for different purposes and different clientele. Some for floors or seat covers, some for entrances or plain ornamentation, some to soften the beds and some for bed covers. Some are made for the poor, some for the middle class, some for the rich and some for the rulers. Most importantly some are made for sale locally, and some for exports, others again on explicit orders.

In studying Indian productions, I have found Jon Thompson's suggestion very useful. Thompson suggests classifying a carpet according to the circumstances and the purpose for which it was made rather than its place of origin.[17] Consequently he suggests the following four categories:

Tribal carpets are not really designed, but are woven directly from memory and they are primarily made for use and not for sale.

For the *cottage industry* weaver, the input on the loom is part-time. They still retain some of the tribal background, but as the production is for sale, they modified their work to suit the buyer's interests. Therefore, they often include ideas from what is fashionable—invariably such ideas also include those the weaver has encountered from towns and cities.

The *town and city workshops* produce for sale, with commercial financing and with division of labour as an important element. Thus, carpets are designed by designers. They introduce the artistic element, make drawings, and colour charts, which that are followed precisely. The skills of the craftsmen employed in the spinning, the dyeing, and knotting determine whether the final product matches the interest and wallet of the buyer, at a satisfactory return for the producer and financer. Unless one deals with a carpet made specifically for order—which was a common practice among wealthy Indians up to World War II—the buyer and those who actually produce the carpet seldom meet. It also seems appropriate to include the present trend of outsourcing the knotting to this category.

On the issue of workshop carpets, Thompson argues that these from an artistic point of view belongs to the category of 'decorative art'. Today this is recognized as genuine art form, and designers are recognized as artists in their own right. He further makes the point that as such the workshop carpets should be judged as art objects by the quality of their designs and execution. Comparing these with carpets of other categories is meaningless as they are produced under completely different parameters.

---
[17] Jon Thompson, *Oriental Carpets: From Tents, Cottages and Workshops of Asia*, 1988.

Court carpets were also produced with high degree of division of labour, and excellence in all areas was demanded. The commercial element was of less significance and the patron provided both sustenance and the material. Patrons own interest in the enterprise would often be a combination of the status such patronage would give; the need to meet their own requirements for floor covers or gifts; or when such needs where satisfied, as exchange for cash or favours. The artist in charge of the production would either discus what carpets to make with the patron or make such decisions on their own. These patronage arrangements—that also prevailed in courts elsewhere in Asia and in Europe—were not restricted to carpets, but applied equally to all manners of arts and crafts. When the relationship between the artist and the patron was that of mutual respect and appreciation, it did produce an excellent environment in which artistic innovations thrived and excellent pieces of art and craft surfaced. In the case of carpet-making this is certainly manifested by the products of the Mughal era, as well as later productions for Indian royalty, aristocrats, and British administrators. In some cases, the artist would be allowed to take on production for other interested parties. Such work could be quite lucrative both for the producer and foreign buyers. Completion of such orders, however, would naturally come second to the demands of the artist's patron.

The patronage system, however, never managed to meet sudden bursts in export demand. This naturally infuriated the merchants in Europe and America who were unable to meet their customer's demands, or promises of delivery. In the wake of the well-known World Exhibition of 1851 this situation quickly led the merchants to direct investment and active involvement in workshops on the subcontinent.

Indian carpets, with some minor exceptions in the Deccan and the traditional Tibetan speaking areas of India, used to belong to one of the two latter categories. Today, the patronage system has long since disappeared and only different types of workshop productions prevails—including those made under an 'outsourcing' scheme or those made on special order. With exception of the simplest of designs, this implies that Indian carpet production was, and is, executed under a regime of extensive division of labour, and should be labelled decorative art and judged as such.

Given the above it is somewhat surprising that Birdwood and Mumford—who both were recognized as authorities in their time—seem to attribute the deteriorations of artistic quality in carpet-making to the fact that weavers have to follow predetermined patters. Particularly as there were good reasons to assume that the highly revered Mughal carpets were made under such a regime.

It is even more surprising that we also today come across literature that makes sweeping statements to the same effect. This is done instead of recognizing that artistically poor carpets—and for that sake carpets with poor material and execution—in most cases are produced in answer to demands from an uniformed market which in addition is unwilling to pay for the real product.

CONTEMPORARY PRODUCTION OF KNOTTED CARPETS

There is no conceivable reason why Indian designers, master craftsmen, and weavers with their traditions and their cost levels should not be able to compete with Iranians in production of quality carpets internationally. Not the least if they can educate the well-to-do upper middle class and the upper classes of this reality, and develop and maintain their internal market. Kunwar Jagdish Prasad is as relevant today as when he in 1907 in similar conditions declared: 'It rests with the Indian public to create a demand for good carpets, and there seems no doubt that the modern workman will not fall very short of his predecessor of the Mughal era.'[18]

---

[18]Kunwar Jagdish Prasad, *Monograph on Carpet Making in the United Provinces*.

BOTEH FROM THE NAWAB OF RAMPUR'S JAIL

Place of production: Most probably Rampur Jail
Year of production: Late nineteenth or early twentieth century
Size: 255 cm x 152 cm (8'5"x5')
Material: Pashmina (Tibetan) wool on cotton warp and woollen weft
Knot: Senneh knots, 144/sq. inch—with a somewhat modified Jaipur back

Being able to acquire a beautiful carpet and present it to guests is in itself a great reward. Having a good story associated with the acquisition can help you retain 'the floor' for some further minutes, which certainly add to the pleasure. Before discussing this particular carpet, I therefore take the liberty of touching on two elements closely associated with it. The first concerns the princely state of Rampur where the carpet most likely was produced, and used. The second is the significance of the central motif of the carpet.

A BIT OF RAMPUR'S HISTORY

The place to which this carpet is attributed has a most interesting, and in some ways sad story to tell. And the Afghan/Pashtun connection might partly explain why Rampur became a recognized carpet producing location in the second half of the nineteenth and first half of the twentieth century.

The princely state of Rampur was a small state located in the northern part of what today is the state of Uttar Pradesh. The state of Rampur was established by Faizullah Khan in October 1774 with encouragement from, and as vassal state of, the famous British East India Company.

Faizullah Khan was one of the chieftains of the Rohilla community with his domain in the Rampur area. The Rohillas were descendants of a 45,000 strong contingence of Pashtun tribes from Afghanistan which came to India as mercenaries. This was at the behest of the Mughal emperor Aurangzeb who needed to quell a Rajput upraising in the very early part of the eighteenth century. Having endeared themselves in the eyes of the emperor they were given large tracks of land in the western part of UP. Here they settled from around 1730 and established their domain in a form of a

Boteh, Rampur Jail
Late nineteenth and early twentieth century
255 x 152 cm (8'5" x 5')

tribal confederacy. This area became known as Rohilkhand (the land of the Rohillas).

With their warrior tradition and increased immigration from Afghanistan the Rohillas soon represented a considerable power—which they exercised. Due to ill fortunes of war combined with lack of diplomacy, however, the major area of Rohilkand was annexed by the more powerful nawab of Oud in 1774, also with assistance of the East India Company. The Rohilla leaders had to flee their capital and take shelter in the jungles.

At the same time as they supported the nawab of Oud in annexing the larger areas of Rohilkand and cut the Rohillas to size, the Company encourage Faizullah Khan to set up a smaller independent Rohilla state in the Rampur area, gave him protection, and recognized him as the nawab with title and prerogatives.

Nawab Faizullah Khan was quite clearly a man of many talents and statesmanship. During turbulent times, he managed to rule his state for the next twenty years and died a natural death. He also had a great interest in education, gave scholarships, and began the collection of Arabic, Persian, Turkish and Urdu manuscripts which now make up the bulk of the Rampur Raza Library. With additions by his descendants this gradually became, and continues even today to be a unique repository of Islamic literature.

Following in his footsteps a number of his successors proved able to handle the challenges of maintaining the semi-autonomy of this small state with a primarily immigrant population. They also initiated reforms and developments in line with its time. The state of Rampur therefore gradually came to play a larger role in the social, political, and cultural life of North India than their size and background should indicate. In this context it naturally did not hurt their cause that they sided with the East India Company during the First War of Independence in 1857.

One of the progressive nawabs of the post 1857 era was Nawab Kalb Ali Khan who ruled from 1865 to 1887. He was literate in Urdu, Arabic, and Persian. He continued to enlarge the collection of literature in his library, did much to uplift standards of education, and instituted reforms in his prisons. He was knighted in Agra by the Prince of Wales, and was a member of Council of the Viceroy—no little merit considering that there probably were more than hundred states larger than Rampur, and thirty-seven who were ranked at the same level or higher. He ruled for more than twenty-two years.[19] His son followed in his footsteps and the *Imperial Gazetteer* of 1909 describes a state in considerable development. With the partition and the changes that followed the majority of

---

[19] *The Imperial Gazetteer*, 1909, Rampur.

both leaders and common members of the tribe were forced to embark on a re-migration—this time into the southern part of Pakistan. Those remaining are, however, against poor odds still fighting to retain their identity. A dramatic and sad destiny for a tough and proud people.

THE SIGNIFICANCE OF THE BOTEH MOTIF

The Boteh has always intrigued those interested in carpet, not the least because it is very popular motif. At the same time one has not been able to conclude on what it really represents. Ian Bennet indicates in his book *Jail Birds: An Exhibition of 19th Century Indian Carpets* that the motif by most writers is considered to have originated in India in the seventeenth century.[20] In that case it would be natural to argue that it represents a mango—an idea I with my Indian background initially thought was the case when I encountered it in a carpet. I am not the one to argue the wisdom of scholars, but wonder if the following arguments put forward by T. H. Harris in 1908 might still be valid:[21]

In his interesting chapter on the symbolism of the oriental carpet Harris refers to the chief interpreter of Shah Nasr-ed-Din who told Mumford that 'the device represents the chief ornament of the old Iranian crown, during one of the earliest dynasties; that the jewel was a composite one, of pear shape, and wrought of so many stones that, viewed from different sides, displayed a great variety of colours.'

And Harris continuous to write: 'If this explanation be correct, it is easy to understand the depth of sentiments connected with it. It is not to be supposed that the shape was chosen for such perpetuity without some real symbolic or religious reason. Taking into consideration the deep devotion to fire and the sun of the ancient Persians, there is no room to believe otherwise than that this crown-jewel shape represents, in its first meaning, the flame which they worshipped, and which is reverently worshiped to this day by their prosperity here in India and in Southern Persia.' Also, Sir Birdwood argued a similar theory. Both these learned men might still be right as far as the original symbolism of the Boteh is concerned.

THE CARPET

I have not been able to identify private businesses producing carpets in Rampur at the turn of the century. Nor that the nawabs ever ran carpet production on the palace premises. The latter would have been surprising, as they could have ordered any carpet of their liking produced in their jail.

---

[20] Ian Bennet, *Jail Birds: An Exhibition of the 19th Century Indian Carpets*.
[21] T. H. Harris, *Monograph on the Carpet weaving Industry of Southern India*, Madras, 1908, p. 57.

While it therefore cannot be ruled out other options, it seems most likely that this carpet was made by inmates in the Rampur Jail.

Given the nawab's cultural interests, his Afghan heritage, and that it already in 1888 is documented production of piled carpets in Rampur Jail, makes it fairly certain that the jail production was initiated already during Nawab Kalb Ali Khan's reign.[22]

The use of Pashmina wool and the quality of design and execution also indicates that this was not a run-of-the-mill production for local sale or export. It rather gives the impression of being a carpet commissioned by an individual who was able to demand, as well as pay the bill. That the carpet has been well maintained for about hundred years, and was disposed of by a person known to have some relations to the former ruling family of Rampur, supports this assumption.

The carpet gives an impression of having been made through a well thought process involving choice of design, material, knotting, and depth of pile. It does not have the heavy feeling associated with many other jail products from North India, and particularly those from Agra. Quite the contrary, the carpet has velvety feel to it, in spite of the foundation basically is what H. K. Wattal terms the 'Jaipur back'. However, it has a considerable degree of 'depressed warp'[23] made of stout cotton. The velvety feel seems intentional and suits the carpet. It is possibly a result of—quite uncommonly in similar quality carpets—using untwisted wool for the second pick of weft. A medium knot count can also contribute. The knot count does, however, not devalue the carpet since the design has taken this into account by avoided use of too fine details, but nevertheless retained its richness.

The main border is marked and breaks with the patterns used in the field of the carpet. An interesting element of the border is that the vines used to tie the palmettes together resembles the fifteenth century Indian Wag-Wag pattern.[24]

The Botehs are positioned regularly and neatly all over the field. They are relatively large and placed with a spacing that allows for inserting stylized leaves and flowers on twigs between them. By this arrangement the designer has created a carpet which depicts peace and harmony, rather than restlessness which in my opinion often is the case in other carpets where the botehs rule the field exclusively.

---

[22]T. N. Mukharji, *Art-manufactures of India*, 1988, p. 390.
[23]Ian Bennet and JohnSiudmak, *Rugs and Carpets of the World*, 1988, Tiger Books International, p. 18; Joyce C. Ware, *The Official Price Guide, Oriental Rugs*, 1992, House of Collectibles, p. 25.
[24]Kamaladevi Chattopadhyaya, *Carpets and Floor Coverings of India*, plate 50.

A HERATI-INSPIRATION FROM AMRITSAR

Place of production: Amritsar workshop
Year of production: 1920s
Size: 180 cm x 122 cm (5'11"x4'1")
Material: Wool on cotton warp and weft
Knot: Senneh knots, 165 sq. inch with a Jaipur back

ABOUT PRODUCTION IN AMRITSAR

Several authors have pointed out that Amritsar—the Holy City of the Sikhs—does not have an ancient heritage in carpet production. Nor do we find documented evidence that any private carpet-making of substance existed in Amritsar prior to establishment of the Devi Sahai Chamba Company in 1860.[25] By the first decade of the twentieth century, however, it had become one of the largest carpet-producing centre in India. Tirthankar Roy attributes the quite phenomenal development to two important factors: First, that the prison in Amritsar well before 1880 had developed a reputation for producing very good carpets. Secondly, that Amritsar already from the beginning of the nineteenth century had a migrant Kashmiri population which were involved in weaving of shawls. When the shawl market crashed many of the weavers shifted to carpet production. One should possibly also add that Amritsar had advantages such as access to good water and good wool from the mountains close by.[26] Roy argues that the entrepreneurs behind this initiative were able to market their products on the strength of the brand name created by the jail. Further that 'with the closure of carpets inside jails, the private industry flourished significantly, in which growth the reputation of jail goods and labour played a role'. At the turn of the century, it was estimated that this production engaged some 5,000 persons. The 'decease' of the market lure, or the pressure of the European and American markets, unfortunately also affected Amritsar. Shoddy design and workmanship became too frequent, leading to loss of reputation. By 1905, however, stability seemed to have been restored, but at a significantly lower production level.

---

[25] Jasleen Dhamija, *Marg*, vol. XVII, no. 4, September 1965, p. 31.
[26] John Kimberly Mumford, *Oriental Rugs*, Charles Scribner's Sons, 1901, p. 259.

This situation continued well up to 1925 with more than 120 looms and 500 men in full-time operation. Possibly as a result of the economic depression in the late 1920s and 30s, production started declining and was dramatically reduced already in 1947. The partition brought the industry close to total standstill. Most of the weavers were Muslims who migrated to Pakistan, and not a single expert weaver was left in Amritsar.[27]

Then, by mid-1970, the industry had again started picking up, but only 100 looms were active in the whole of Punjab.[28] Today the production in Amritsar is back up and running, and while not producing top-shelf products the carpets are good value for money.[29]

Amritsar has always been associated with the Mouri pattern which originally came from Merv in Central Asia, but generally been a centre producing to the demands of the market. It should also be noted that Amritsar—as a result of the influence of Kashmiri weavers—was the second region to start using the Talim in their production process.

THE CARPET

This is a well-made carpet with a rather unusual design, but not likely unique as one finds a very similar pattern in a carpet produced in Bhadohi many years later. In spite of the latter being around fifty years younger it is likely that both designers have had another carpet as their inspiration.[30] Possibly one from the *Vienna Catalogue*.

The foundation is that of the Jaipur Back, but as in the case of the carpet attributed to Rampur the warp and weft is not completely covered by the pile, and the second pick of weft shows as a continuous vertical line on the back of the carpet.[31]

It also has an unusual colour scheme. It is known that workshops in Amritsar produced carpets on orders from American and European clients and therefore often were at odds with Indian or Persian tradition. This carpet, however, gives an 'Indian impression'. This assumption is supported by the fact that it has remained in India.

---
[27]Ibid.
[28]Tirthankar Roy, *Traditional Industry in the Economy of Colonial India*, pp. 207, 215–16, and Jasleen Dhamija.
[29]Andrew Middleton, *Rugs & Carpets*, 1996.
[30]E. Ganz-Ruedin, *Indian Carpets*, Thames and Hudson, 1984.
[31]H. K. Wattal, *Marg*, vol. xviii, September 1965, p. 41.

A Potential Jailbird Design, Jaipur Central Jail
Early 20th century
223 x 146 cm (7'42 x 4'10")

GRAPES AND FLOWERS FROM A WORKSHOP IN JAIPUR

Place of production: Workshop in Jaipur
Year of production: 1975-1980
Size: 180 cm x 122 cm (5'11"x4'1")
Material: Good wool on a rather thin cotton warp and two strands of thin weft
Knot: Senneh knots with 121 knots/ sq. inch

Much of existing literature on Indian carpets claims that the production in the Jaipur area is of relatively new date. There is, however, documentation indicating that both wool and silk carpets were produced in a workshop at Amber Fort already in the seventeenth century. This production, unfortunately, seems to have been of rather short duration. From this time and onwards no information has so far been found relating to production of piled carpet in the Jaipur area until Maharaja Sawai Ram Singh, the ruler of the state of Jaipur, revitalized the art by introducing it to inmates in the Jaipur Central Jail around 1856.[32]

In the latter part of the nineteenth century, Sir Birdwood strongly condemned the practice of carpet-making as part of the work regime in the jails on the subcontinent.[33] The effort of the rulers in introducing carpet production in Jaipur Central Jail, however, seems to have laid the basis upon which the revival of a private production could grow and develop from the very beginning of the twentieth century.

The revival has gradually matured and come to employ thousands of artisans producing sound products in the Jaipur area today. This 'free' production included piled woollen and cotton carpets, as well as dhurries. It is also documented that the House of the Golechas—a local firm—manufactured carpets as one of the first entrepreneurs moving into this field. These were considered to be of very good quality and with knot counts of between 250 and 400/sq. inch.[34] Other companies followed, and at one time in the late 1930s there were as many as fifty factories producing piled carpets

---
[32]See also chapter on Indian jail carpets.
[33]Sir George Birdwood, *The Industrial Arts of India*, 1884.
[34]Chattopadhyay, *Carpets and Floor Coverings of India*.

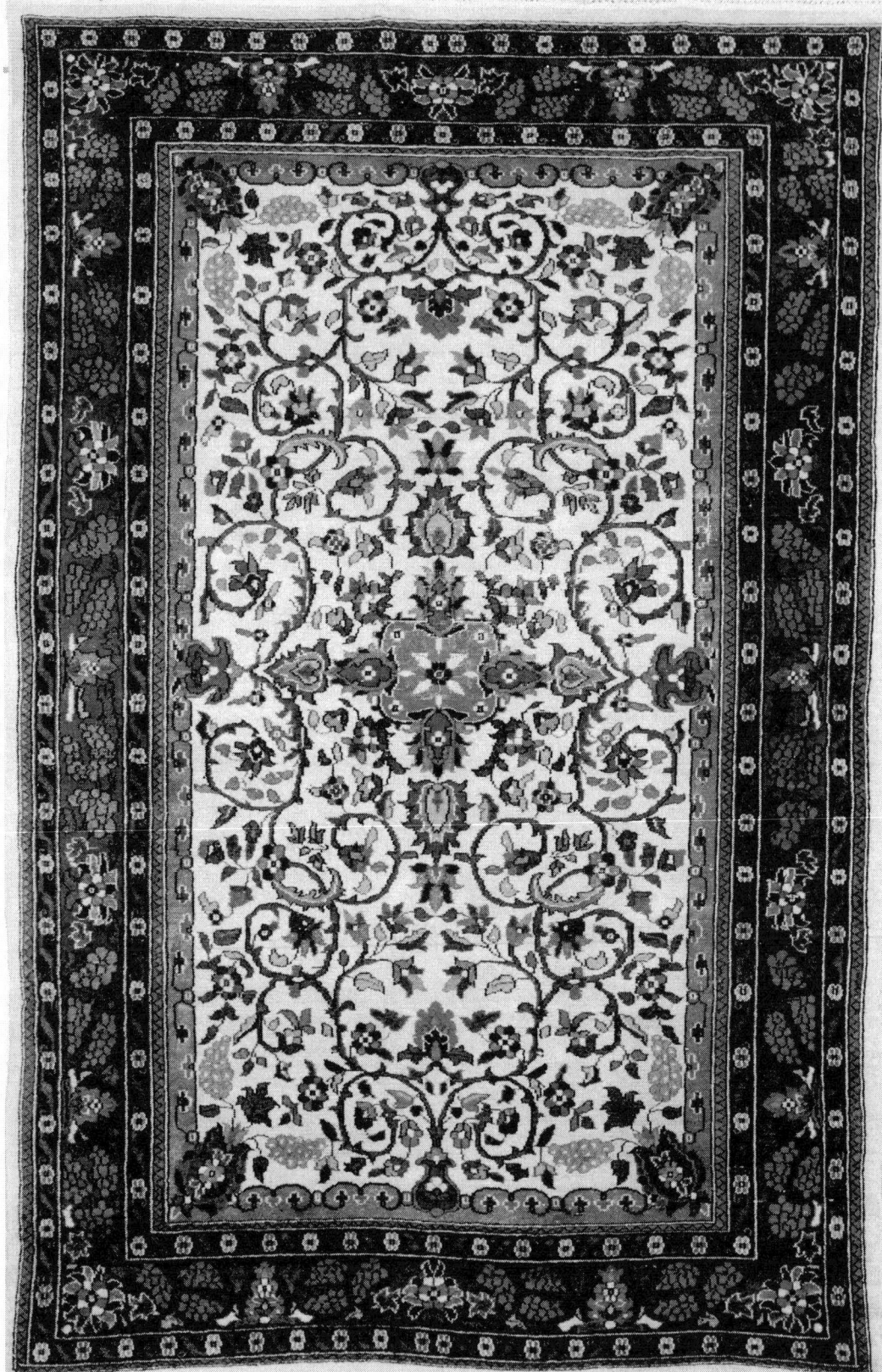

Jaipur Free Workshop 1975–80
180 x 122 cm (5'11" x 4'1")

in Jaipur. However, many actors were financed by speculators who had scant regard for quality control, or market saturation. This resulted in a crisis which culminated in the 1950s, and in the early 1960s only a handful factories were left in operation.[35]

As in many other carpet producing areas in India, the Jaipur producers showed ability to bounce back. Already in 1976 Chattopadhyay states that a new revival was in the making. Today the private manufacturing has been re-established, and carpets are made for both export and the domestic markets that are good value for money. Some of the workshops are undoubtedly also capable of producing top quality products of artistic value, if the market so demands.

This carpet is probably produced in the early part of the 'second revival period'. It is not an expensive production, showing the characteristics of being made in what H. K. Wattal calls the Mirzapur back.[36]

The design is, however, pleasing and the complexity and details are adjusted to fit the fairly low knot account. My impression is that Jaipur production from the 1980s tended to stay close to, and even copy Persian patterns—most probably a result of 'customer's choice'. While it carries a strong Persian influence this carpet also has a distinctive 'Indian feel', and a more typical Indian colour combination than the majority of the carpets produced in Jaipur at that time. It is also different to those marketed presently, where the design tends to show a closer affinity to patterns from the old jail productions. But precisely for those reasons no less interesting or pleasing.

---

[35] Asha Rani Mathur: p. 57.
[36] Marg vol XVIII Sept. 1965, H.K. Wattal: Technical Survey of the Carpet Industry, p. 41.

4
About Kashmir and its Carpets

When writing anything about Kashmir it is unavoidable not to touch upon its beautiful lushness, its lake and forests, its springs and wild rivers, or the majestic scenery of its snow-capped mountains. It is also difficult to believe that this nature has not made a profound influence on its rich culture of poetry, music, religious traditions, paintings, or the decorative art built into its handicrafts. There can be little doubt that Kashmir—if it can avoid the repetitive political turbulences—rapidly can regain its position as one of India's most sought-after travel destinations. One can only hope that Kashmir's politicians and bureaucrats already have clear plans and regulations in place to ensure that the development that follows such a status improves, rather than deteriorate, its environment. If this could be the case the state could avoid the fate of so many of the other hill stations on the subcontinent.

A BIT OF KASHMIRI HISTORY AND ITS CARPET PRODUCTION

As mentioned earlier there are documented evidence that the art and craft of knotted carpets was introduced to the valley in the very early part of the fifteenth century by Sultan Zain-ul-Abadin. He had as the prince of Kashmir—some years prior to ascending the throne—spent seven years under detention in Samarkand. Here he had come to appreciate the art of carpet-making. On his return to the valley, he therefore brought with him skilled craftsmen, and also imported weavers from Persia to train local artisans. The production, however, depended on his patronage and, after Sultan Zain-ul-Abadin's demise, his successors did not continue his interest, and production of carpets went into oblivion.

It only received its revival in 1615 after a troubled period in Kashmir's history was replaced by relative calm when Kashmir was annexed into the Mughal empire and Ahmed Beg Khan was deputed as governor of Kashmir by Emperor Jahangir. With his patronage and the initiative of a Kashmiri merchant production was restarted. A strong interest in, and patronage of, carpet production by the emperors Jahangir and Shah Jahan also contributed significantly. This, however, also coincided with a considerable interest among the wealthy of Europe, thereby creating a market for the products beyond that of the rulers and their courts.

This last initiative gave a new boost to carpet-making in Kashmir. The organization of production changed with introduction of master craftsmen (vasta-ustad) heading the workshops (karkhanas) and supervising the work of craftsmen (tsats) and the apprentices (shadgirds). Systems of wages were introduced in place of payment in kind.[1] Both imperial and private karkhanas seems to have been in operation and thriving from around 1620.[2]

Compared to most other areas of India, Kashmir was in a good position to exploit the increased demands. The region has a climate contributing to a local market for woollen products and a local supply of wool. Kashmir had already in the seventeenth century, developed an excellent tradition and competence in spinning, dyeing and weaving of fine woollen products. It further had a location in which its people naturally had contact with other groups with carpet traditions, and therefore would have retained a small base of indigenous artisans. In this period Kashmir also became the sole importer of pashmina wool from its source in western Tibet. This was a material that attracted the interest of Emperor Akbar who is said to have had it tested for dyeing. It gradually became the material of choice for production of the finest carpets of that period. According to Daniel Walker: 'The finest of Indian carpets of all, and really the finest of all classical carpets from any culture, are the pieces made with the pile of pashmina wool—the undercoat of the Himalayan mountain goat.'[3]

Given the above it is not surprising to note the number of carpets with probable attribution to Kashmir that were awarded a place in the Metropolitan Museum's exhibition 'Flower Underfoot: Indian Carpets of the Mughal Era'—an exhibition that aimed at representing the highest level of achievement in carpet-making.

Based on the research associated with this exhibition, as well as other resent work, there are good reasons to claim that the artists and artisans of Kashmir participated significantly in developing the Mughal style of carpets, and produced these at a significant, but not large scale for a period that stretched from early seventeenth century to mid-eighteenth century. Thereafter the valley unfortunately again faced political turmoil due to decline of the power of the Mughal empire. As in other parts of the empire, however, this decline gradually led to the growth of strong regional rulers. Many of these potentates took over and continued the patronage of arts in their areas. They imported weavers into their domains where they continued the production with the local dignitaries as their customers, and probably also English and French residents. This situation seems to have

---

[1]Jaya Jaitly, *Crafts of Jammu, Kashmir & Ladakh*, Ahmedabad: Mapin, p. 83.
[2]Daniel Walker, *Flowers Underfoot: Indian Carpets of the Mughal Era*, Thames and Hudson, 1998 p.113.
[3]Ibid.

continued for a period up to the end of the eighteenth century, and included Kashmir. Not surprising it also became the period when the Indo-Isfahan style gradually yielded to a more independent style with less Persian influence.[4]

Unfortunately, this was at the same time a period of more or less continuous turmoil in Kashmir. That production in Kashmir was able to continue tells considerable about the resilience of its people. The erosion of Mughal power led to misrule by its governors and finally to an Afghan invasion and annexation of Kashmir in 1752. Rather than what the people of Kashmir had hoped for, this invasion led to more exploitation and terror—first under the Afghans for the following sixty-seven years, and thereafter twenty-seven not much better years under Sikh rule.

By the mid-eighteenth century when tumultuous times again struck Kashmir, however, there are reasons to believe that carpet production had become a natural and ingrained element of Kashmiri arts and crafts. Good quality carpets—on a very limited scale—continued to be produced for local dignitaries and foreign residents in India. Kashmir therefore was one of the few remaining centres of carpet production on the subcontinent in the early part of the nineteenth century.

That a limited production still must have continued and turned out valuable carpets during the first half of the nineteenth century was demonstrated by the interest Kashmiri carpets aroused at the Great Exhibition of 1851. Among other fine specimens, Kashmir presented a carpet with 700 knots/sq. inch. This carpet had been presented as a gift to the newly installed maharaja of Kashmir, and attracted deserved attention. The London Exhibition brought about much activity and revived the industry in India generally. Most of the areas where activity had remained, these were now being reactivated.[5]

Kashmir had as recently as 1848 come under British administration with a new ruler. Maharaja Gulag Singh was a man of considerable talents and great determination who ensured law and order, and laid the foundation of the modern Jammu and Kashmir state. He brought under his control the various areas that originally was looked upon as part of the state, but which had never really known any settled government. By the time of his death in 1857, he had ensured peace and sound administration in an area about the size of Switzerland. Fortunately, he in turn was succeeded by rulers who introduced the rule of law, and continued his modernisation and development efforts.

These latter political changes naturally also benefitted the carpet industry. The industry was

---
[4]Roy, *Traditional Industry in the Economy of Colonial India*, p. 200.
[5]Black, *Worlds Rugs & Carpets*.

reinvigorated by local and foreign entrepreneurs. Already in 1850, Mitchell & Company was encouraged to establish itself in the valley. This company is credited with introducing and organizing a stable production, which secured a steady flow to Western markets.[6] In addition, Watt, in his writing on the Delhi Exhibition in 1903, commends the company with the following reference: 'The firm of Mitchell & Co. sent only a few rugs, but these were very charming, perhaps the best woven and most artistically coloured of any Indian rugs in the Exhibition'. The following paragraphs of his deliberations indicates that one reason for Watt's praise was that these carpets—in contrast to much of the other productions exhibited—were not mere copies of Persian designs.[7]

By 1888, C. M. Hadow, East Indian Carpet Company, and several local firms had established workshops and exported to other parts of the subcontinent, to Europe and USA. This ensured that Kashmir from mid-nineteenth century and in the following five to six decades dominated the export of fine carpets from the subcontinent. Kashmiri carpets won distinction and praise at every international exhibition they participated, including Chicago Expo in 1893, Paris in 1900, London 1902, 1903, and 1906.[8] As a result of the attention it received the industry in Kashmir undoubtedly grew considerably during this period, but reliable records are hard to come by.

The size of the carpet industry in Kashmir was, however, always heavily dependent on the export market, both in the subcontinent, as well as abroad. The production therefore to a significant extent depended on the world economy and world politics. As a consequence, the recession in Europe and USA in the 1920s gave a setback to the industry in the valley. As the world economy again picked up also the Kashmiri production was revitalized. By 1931, there were as many as 715 looms with approximately 3,000 weavers in operation in Srinagar. This level of activity seems to have continued until the advent of World War II. The war took most of the strength out of the market for fine carpets, and the following partition of India and Kashmir reduced both the number of artisans as well as those willing to invest in the state. By 1947, the equivalent figures were down to some 200 looms and 750 weavers.[9] This naturally inhibited Kashmir's ability to fully exploit the new affluence that gradually surfaced in other parts of the world in the 1950s and 1960s. In spite of this, a census in 1960 recorded more than 1,500 weavers and 350 ancillary workers in activity, and the numbers were increasing. The tourists flocking into the valley are said to have contributed significantly to increased production during this period.[10]

---

[6]Chattopadhyaya, *Carpets and Floor Coverings of India*.
[7]Watt, *Delhi Exhibition*, p. 431.
[8]Chattopadhyaya, *Carpets and Floor Coverings of India*, p, 34; also Younghusband, *Kashmir*, 1915.
[9]Roy, *Traditional Industry in the Economy of Colonial India*, p. 215.
[10]*Marg*, September 1965, p. 35.

REFLECTIONS ON CONTEMPORARY KASHMIRI PRODUCTION

Probably because of renewed disturbances in the valley, or a depressed market, the number of weavers did not increase significantly in the years prior to 1985. However, the general boost in export of Indian carpets that occurred in the late part of the 1980s also benefitted the workshops in Kashmir and resulted in an increased production. At this time there are also indications that the larger workshops started 'outsourcing' their production to smaller workshops and individual weavers by providing designs, material and monetary advances in the same manner as is the practice in Mirzapur or Qom in Iran.

In spite of the repeated turbulence in Kashmir over the last two decades carpet production has continued to grow, but in leaps and bonds. Contributing factors for this erratic development were competition from other centres where government support had been more effective; the negative impact of 9/11 when a fall in the orders of 80 per cent was recorded;[11] and the world recession from 2008.

At a peak before the recession around 250,000 people were engaged in the industry, but the number dwindled to somewhere around 100,000 in the beginning of 2011[12]. By mid-2011 production was again picking up. This was partly due to the markets improving, and partly because the state government was taking an active interest. The industry anticipates a continued growth.

When tracing the modern history of Kashmiri carpet production, it is clear that the industry not only has suffered from external and internal economic and political turmoil. On many occasions its suffering has been a consequence of actions from within, from the greed and unethical business practices of the few, to the determent of the many. In the early periods it was those that showed carpets of top quality when seeking an order, but shipped consignments with carpets containing 'chunnam wool' (wool from dead animals removed with caustic soda); those that in latter part of nineteenth century replaced vegetable dyes with aniline dyes without checking the consequences and certainly without informing the buyer; or those who in the 1980s—when Kashmiri carpets generally was strengthening its reputation—substituted mesmerized cotton for good silk. In all these cases it was the fly-by-night operators who spoiled the market for the serious actors. A cursory glance through popular carpet literature is enough to see how much damage such actions of the few has caused the earnings of the industry as a whole, and not least its designers and weavers.[13]

---

[11]Overseas Kashmiri magazine.
[12]Zubair Ahmad, *Kashmir Life*, vol. 3, issue 11, May 2011.
[13]Birdwood, *Industrial Arts*; Jaitly, *Crafts of Jammu, Kashmir and Ladakh*, p. 84.

From the mid-1990s onwards, it is the author's impression that the industries effort to protect their own image and 'remove the bad eggs from the basket' has had a positive impact, and that the above practices are becoming a thing of the past. The US has also removed the mandatory 'child labour free' certificate in recognition of the work done to reduce the level of forced labour in the carpet sector.[14] Hopefully this will be the end of a practice which with good reason has haunted the Indian—including the Kashmiri—production since the nineteenth century.

The Kashmiri carpet industry has, however, also suffered from sweeping negative statements in popular, as well as in some that present itself as academic literature. They can generally be summed into three issues.

- First, the claim that Kashmiri carpets are poor in quality of material and workmanship;

- Secondly, that they are produced for commerce and in workshops with high degree of division of labour and therefore cannot be considered art;

- And finally, that they are mere copies or imitations of Iranian and Central Asian designs, have no identity of their own, and consequently no artistic value.

Since my experience indicates that these types of statements have had, and continue to have, an impact on the reputation of Kashmiri production generally they warrant some deliberation.

That Daniel Walker[15] tends to favour Kashmir as the origin of a number of the superb carpets from mid-seventeenth as well as the number of recognitions Kashmiri carpets in latter part of the nineteenth and early twentieth century received contradicts the first statement in a historic perspective. That this tradition has continued during the twentieth century is confirmed by several authors.[16] As mentioned earlier, however, some modern Kashmiri carpets of lower grades and made for export have not maintained the quality one would expect. In spite of this and after having gone through pile after pile of Kashmiri carpets over the last twenty years I would, so far as material and workmanship is concerned, second the words of Asha Rani Mathur when she in 2004 states that Kashmir has the finest production in India. I would also dare to claim that Jasleen Dhamija's statement from 1965 that high grade Kashmiri carpets can compare with the very best of the Persian products remains as true today—if not more so.

---

[14]One World South Asia 30.9.2011.
[15]Walker, *Flowers Underfoot*, p. 112.
[16]Dhamija 1965, E. Gans-Ruedin 1984, K. Chattopadhyaya 1976, Asha Rani Mathur 2004.

In a discourse related to the second claim it is natural to draw inspiration from Jon Thompson[17]—who as mentioned in the general chapter on Indian carpets[18]—argues for a basic classification of carpet according to the circumstances under and, one might add, the purpose for which they are made, rather than its place of origin. When using these classifications Kashmiri carpet making was initially introduced in the form of court or patronage production. During the revival of the 'industry' in the Mughal period there are indications that 'workshop production' for commercial purposes was introduced.[19] This gradually took over as the manner in which carpets are made.

On the issue of workshop carpets Thompson argues that these carpets from an artistic point of view belongs to the category of 'decorative art', and that designers should be recognized as artists in their own right. Since Kashmiri carpets, nearly without exception, are workshop products the manner in which the production takes place should not in itself warrant a statement that they are derived of artistic value. On the contrary many of the carpets that were produced in Kashmiri workshops during the Mughal era are, as previously indicated, regarded as the most artistic and aesthetic of all times. This certainly supports Thompson's claim that the workshop carpets should 'be judged as art objects by the quality of their design, and not compared to carpets of fundamentally dissimilar character such as those woven from memory'.

Those who claim that Kashmiri designs are mere copies or imitations of designs from Iran tend to forget or hide that close economic and cultural associations have existed between Kashmir and parts of Persia and Central Asia for a thousand years, and that carpet-making was introduced into the valley by Central Asian and Persian artists and artisans. Also when carpet-making was revived in late fifteenth century Persian carpet-makers where 'imported' for re-establishing training and production. As carpet-making has been a living element of the arts and crafts of Kashmir since that time it seems both legitimate and quite natural that carpet designs in Kashmir even today show a strong adherence to their heritage. When considering how beliefs, ideas, symbols, and fashions have travelled back and forth over centuries in these regions one cannot but feel that the derogative manner with which these statements often are pronounced only can stem from a lack understanding of historic and cultural developments.

The royal workshop in Srinagar was an important contributor to the development of the 'Mughal designs'. It is therefore relevant to ponder why that tradition did not become more pronounced

---

[17]Jon Thompson, Oriental Carpets – From Tents, Cottages and Workshops of Asia 1988,
[18]See p. 30.
[19]Jasleen Damija, *Marg*, Vol. XVIII September 1965 p. 35.

in the patterns developed when carpet manufacturing on a larger scale was revived after the Great Exhibition of 1851. Watt's comments in connection with carpets at the Delhi Exhibition in 1902 might provide some light on this question when he laments the negative impact the famous publication on Oriental Carpets by the Imperial and Royal Austrian Commercial Museum, had on the indigenous designs.[20] The reason most probably was that the return to more traditional Persian style was in response to demands of the market, and designs in the Persian tradition where assumed to be those that best answered these requirements. And, as mentioned above Kashmiri carpets have always been made either for patrons or for commercial purposes.

There is ample documentation similar to the one mentioned above which confirming that Kashmiri carpet workshops copied Persian carpets in the period from 1851 onwards, and by all likelihood well before that time. However, also carpets from the Mughal era or other parts of India have been objects of the same treatment if they stood the test of time and attracted interest in the market. It might possibly be a surprise to those that sweepingly dismiss Kashmiri carpets for the reasons mentioned above, that also Persian workshops have copied other Persian carpets and lo and behold even Indian carpets with extremely good results.[21] In drawing parallels and being provocative, one could ask if a late number in a limited print of a famous graphic artist has less artistic or aesthetic value than one with an earlier number? What can be reasonable in this connection is to criticize when a copy is poorly executed, or it is marketed as an original.

For the most parts, however, what is being criticized are not Kashmiri copies of Persian carpets, but Kashmiri designs developed with a base in traditional Persian carpets. The relevance of such criticism is as mentioned above questionable. Secondly, an artistic design process normally implies drawing ideas and inspiration from other sources as well as from once own heritage—which in the case of Kashmiri carpet making is Persian. In this process it is recognized that Kashmiri designers or master weavers already from the sixteenth century started introducing typical Kashmiri elements into their carpets. Thirdly this practice has been and still is common in the carpet industry, most certainly also in Iran.[22] Given the above, the use of the term 'Persian imitations' in sweeping description of Kashmiri carpets seems quite unfounded—particularly when the word imitation in this context and in modern English has a derogative connotation.

During research into, and multiple hours of browsing through Kashmiri carpets at regular intervals

---

[20] Watt, *Delhi Exhibition*.
[21] Ibid.
[22] Jon Thompson: Oriental Carpets p. and David Black: World Rugs & Carpets, 1985 p. 71.

over the past twenty years, I have been struck by the ability of the Kashmiri industry to ride the bad waves. They have had to adjust their production to market demands, but in most cases managed this without depriving their products of its basic Kashmiri identity, and then gradually reclaim their ground. I would therefore venture the opinion that Kashmiri workshops in present times produce carpets in the fine segment that are both artistically interesting, have excellent workmanship, and good value for money.

The industry has also through ups and downs been able to, in this day and age of mass production, maintain the knowledge and expertise of what an excellent carpet demands of artistic design, quality of material, and workmanship in execution. Give a reputed workshop in Kashmir an indication of what you are looking for, talk with the designers, give the time required, and you will still by all likelihood receive a masterpiece. But be aware that this is the 'court and patron approach' to carpet production and that uniqueness and quality comes with a price, here as in any form of art.

When evaluating contemporary Kashmiri production, it should, however, also be borne in mind that the Kashmiri workshops have to satisfy different export markets as well as their home market when the carpets are designed. And what a rich Indian would find pleasing in his mansion is not necessarily what I would appreciate in my home in Northern Europe, and vice versa.

My statement above must, however, not be misconstrued as implying that all Kashmiri carpets are worth the label of art, nor are good value for money. The same care and attention must be taken when purchasing Kashmiri carpets as those employed when contemplating carpets from any other carpet producing region. I do, however, hope that the above deliberation would encourage those contemplating buying a carpet to review all options—not the least that of Kashmiri carpets—and make their choices without being intimidated neither by salespeople or writers of carpet literature.

SHORT DESCRIPTION ON TECHNICAL ISSUES

As mentioned earlier, the carpets in Kashmir are workshop productions, and thus involve a high degree of 'division of labour'.

The designer is the artist that determines the pattern and colours of the carpet. The designer should ideally also be able to prescribe the material to be used since the type of yarn—whether it is silk, wool, or cotton—to a considerable degree dictates what patterns can be executed. Good designers are few in number and hard to come by. Without the designers no new designs can be introduced, and consequently they are often those that control the activity.

Between the designer and the weaver, the Kashmir producers have a talim writer. The talim writer translate the designer's prescription for design, cartoons (a cartoon is a full-size paper drawing that is squared, each square representing one knot of a particular colour), and colours schemes into coded strips of paper which is given to the master weaver in a workshop, or to the individual weavers. In the mid-nineteenth century a considerable slump occurred in the market for Kashmir shawls. This coincided with an increased interest for Kashmiri carpets and led to a considerable number of shawl weavers taking up carpet weaving. These weavers were accustomed to weaving intricate patterns using the talim as the method for transferring the designer's instruction of pattern and colours to the weaver. The talim is basically a strip of paper which in code informs of the number of knots and colours to be applied in a vertical line across the carpet. With the new entrants of weavers preferring this method the carpet industry in Kashmir quickly adopted and developed this mode of communication. Preparing the talim is a detailed and time-consuming process which demands close cooperation between the designer and the talim writer. A carpet of 300 cm x 200 cm and a knot count of some 370/sq. inch will require 800 strips for a carpet with a continuous pattern.

The use of the talim later spread to Amritsar where migrant weavers from Kashmir dominated the production. There are indications that use of the talim now is further spreading to other weaving centres in India.

For top quality carpets the general impression is that hand-spun yarn is preferable. For such production accomplished spinners are required, but these days mill-spun yarns are normally used unless a workshop has taken a special order. Similarly, also the dye determines the quality of a carpet. In spite of considerable improvements in chemical dyes there is still a general view that yarn dyed with natural dyes by good dyers can lift a carpet from fine to excellent. Securing accomplished dyers is therefore necessary for a workshop that targets the upper end of the market.

There is a need for master weavers to assign weavers to their tasks depending upon their skills, supervise, and provide quality control. Finally, workshop production would normally imply expertise in sharing and washing of the carpet before it is ready for the market.

Kashmir producers have over the past years increasingly concentrated on carpets with silk pile for quality carpets made in their Persian tradition. Good blends of local and imported wool are still used, but normally for the line of production that is based on their Central Asian heritage. As in the past Pashmina wool tends to be the preferred choice for the most exclusive products.[23] Fortunately

---

[23] Walker, *Flowers Underfoot*, p. 22.

the use of artificial silk and mesmerised cotton seems to be going out of use. One can only hope that the time soon comes when these materials disappear from Kashmiri carpet production totally—in the same way as aniline dye did in the beginning of the twentieth century.[24] Most Kashmiri carpets are made with cotton warp and weft, but silk has become more common in carpets with silk pile.

The quality of a carpet in terms of durability as well as how it feels depends on its foundation, the type of knot used, and the number of knots per square area. All piled carpets from Kashmir use the Senneh or asymmetrical knot, but with three variations. The firmness, thickness, and appearance of the back of the carpet are characteristic features. The variations used in India are usefully described by H. K. Wattal in the well-known Indian art magazine *Marg*.[25]

The most common variation is the Jaipur or Panalidar back. This is created in 'plain weave' by the use of rows of knots tied between adjacent pairs of weft and to adjacent pair of relatively stout warp threads. This is in India today popularly termed single knot. To this is applied a stout twisted first pick weft and a thin soft untwisted and loosely laid second pick of weft. All the first pick of weft lies strait, on top of one half of the of the warp threads and under the other half, and is locked into place by the second pick of weft. Almost one and a half of length of the width of the carpet is used for the second pick of weft. This shows a back with relatively pronounced ribs running the length of a carpet, fully covered with pile yarn. According to Wattal this is the variation which has been, and still is used for the best of Indian carpets.

The other variation which is generally used for carpets in the Central Asian tradition (Kashmiri Bokharas) is a refined version of the Mirzapur back. The Mirzapur back 'is a smooth back without pronounced ribs. It is a thin tough firm back. There is not much disparity in thickness between the first and second weft and neither is very stout. Neither of these lies quite strait and each bends in and out to allow the weft to lie straight, all in the same plane. The warp is completely concealed, but the weft is seen as stripes running across the back. Since each knot of pile appears as two pebbles on the back, where the pile yarn goes round the two warp yarns, the carpet presents a deceptive appearance of fineness on the reverse'. In the Kashmiri version the number of knots of pile in a length of the carpet is nearly twice that of the width. This gives the carpet an extremely supple feel. These carpets are, however, not very stable on the floor and benefits from the use some sort of underfelt.

A sub-variation of the two variations is when the knot is tied to two adjacent pair of warp popularly termed a 'jufti knot'. When this knot is used in Kashmir it is in lower grade carpets as it is regarded

---

[24]George Watt and Percy Brown, *Indian Art and Crafts*, Official Catalogue of Indian Art exhibition, Delhi 1904.
[25]H. K. Wattal, *Marg*, vol. xviii, no. 4, September 1965, p. 41.

to produce less durable products. Wattal's opinion, however, is that it does no harm to the carpet if a competent weaver executes the work properly, and interestingly this knot is somewhat of a 'hallmark of the carpets of Khorasan, the original home of the weavers who later immigrated to India'.[26]

In Kashmiri carpets the number of knots per square is an important indication of the quality. These days it is rare to find quality carpets with knot counts below 225 knots/inch (35/sq. cm.) Knot counts of 324 to 500/sq. inch would be found in fine carpets. However, on a special order some small carpets with silk warp, weft and pile were made in Kashmir in 1984 with knot counts of more than 2700/sq. inch.[27]

---

[26]Walker, *Flowers Underfoot*, p. 27.
[27]Ruedin, *Indian Carpets*, p. 165.

THE LION AND DRAGON CARPET

Place of production: Kashmir
Year of production: Probably third quarter of the twentieth century
Size: 178 cm x 122 cm (5'10" x 4')
Material: Wool on cotton warp and weft
Knot: Senneh knots, 289/sq. inch woven in Jaipur back
Dye: Natural dyes

Given the age of this carpet; its design; the relative high knot count; and its quality of execution it is safe to assume that it must have been commissioned by a very well-to-do and devoted Muslim. And the state of its maintenance—after nearly a century and a half—indicates that it has been kept in reverence. It certainly is not a common piece made for export.

The use of the classical Persian vase pattern as the central motif in the arch (mihrab) of Kashmiri prayer carpets are quite common, and is depicted in a great variety of sophistication—from the most simple to those befitting the well to do and pious.

The design and execution of the mihrab here certainly belongs to the latter category. Each individual element, such as the basic form of the vase, the trees on either side, as well as the flowers, snakes and birds that fill the opening of the prayer arch is shown naturalistically and in great detail.

The most striking element of the carpet, however, is found on the top of the arch. Here—on each side—and between the devotees and the garden of peace—a fierce struggle to death is ongoing. A lion—which in Kashmir signifies the brave and powerful—has its teeth locked into the middle of a dragon-like creature, while the dragon has its teeth in the back of the lion, blood streaming to all sides. The whole battle is accompanied by a screaming parrot. Quite dramatic to be part of a prayer carpet, but at the same time quite appropriate if the idea is to describe the difference between the present and afterlife.

Prayer Carpet – Kashmiri
Third quarter nineteenth century

THE PAULSEN CARPET: LEOPARDS AND DRAGONS

Place of production: Kashmir
Year of production: Turn of the nineteenth and twentieth century
Size: 209 cm x 150 cm (6'10" x 5'1")
Material: Wool on cotton warp and weft;
Knot: Senneh knots, 15x15 =225/sq. inch, woven in Jaipur back
Dye: Natural dyes

During a visit of some friends in 1992, Mr Sayeed brought a pair of 'twin carpets' which he had recently acquired. The term twin carpets indicate that the carpets are made from the same talim and are produced in parallel. These carpets were of Kashmiri origin and in Mr Sayeed's estimation, produced some time in the very early part of the twentieth century. As was the norm, Mr Sayeed left the carpets with us. After having studied them for a few days—which one should always have the opportunity to do—our friends decided to purchase both. This they did, and one of them is shown here. Had they not done so, I would have been first in line, as they had an interesting and rather intense design, and even if quite worn was even and without tears or repairs.

They have a beautiful field with an elegant medallion filled with blue-grey vines and flowers on a bluish background, and surrounded by an aura of rusty pink. Between the aura and the border lays a field of twigs, flowers, antelopes, leopards, and possibly wolves woven inside a nearly continuous ring of 'cloud bands'. This composition of the field is, however, in no way unique. Basically, the same composition is found in the carpet presented in the following pages. It is further used in two carpets from 1980 presented by E. Gans-Ruedin's in his book *Indian Carpets*.[28] When viewing these four carpets together one gains an impression that they all have been designed—not as copies of—but with inspiration from the same source.

Given the style it is natural to seek such a base among Persian carpets. Unfortunately, a browsing through my own collection of carpet literature gave up no such a treasure. Sir Henry Watt's has, however, in 1903 made the observation that 'Perhaps half of the carpets shown at (Delhi) Exhibition

---
[28]Gans-Ruedin, *Indian Carpets*, pp. 179 and 196.

Leopard and Dragons – Kashmiri
Late nineteenth century
209 x 155 cm (6'10" x 5'1")

has been copied from the famous book on Oriental Carpets published by the Imperial and Royal Austrian Commercial Museum.' He further continues to lament that this literature from 1896 has exercised greater influence on the trade than the authors can have envisaged, and was used in carpet centres all over India. While it has raised the standard of Indian production, it has also been injurious by destroying the distinctions that formally existed between the centres.[29]

Consequently, I sought a possible 'base design' from among the carpets presented in that documentation. Not surprisingly a plate of such carpet was indeed found.[30] While this does not provide irrefutable evidence, it certainly makes it likely that this 'Vienna' plate has been the inspiration for all the above designs—of which these twin carpets come closest to the 'original'.

Even in this case 'Indian modifications' have been introduced. The scripts dominating the borders have been exchanged with beds of delicately coloured flowers and the antelopes have become Indian. What seems to contribute to make the presentation more intense, bordering on the sinister, is that the base colour of field is shown in a dark blue colour—rather than white—and the cloud bands surrounding the palmettes on the longitudinal axis in this version are made more prominent than in the original and depicted as fierce-looking dragons.

While recognizing that beauty is in the eyes of the beholder, I would venture that the designer through these adjustments created a set of carpets that are both more natural and more balanced than the one that likely represented his inspiration.

The dragon detail

---

[29] Sir Henry Watt, Official Catalogue of the Delhi Exhibition, p. 431.
[30] C. Purdon Clark, *Oriental Carpets*, vol. i, p. 5n.

THE ANGEL AND BAPTISMAL CARPET

Place of production: Kashmir
Time of production: Turn of the nineteenth and twentieth century
Size: 292 cm x 210 cm (9'7" x 6'11")
Material: Wool on cotton warp and weft;
Knot: Senneh knots, 14x12 =168/sq. inch, woven in Jaipur back
Dye: Natural dyes

When Mr Sayeed, as on many previous occasions, called and informed me that he had found a 'Mitchelson carpet' from the turn of the century I wondered what this would turn out to be. During the following meeting and discussion over the carpet I naturally enquired what he meant by this term. While he had come across several old carpets, which in Kashmir were attributed to this name, he was unsure of its background, but had been made to understand this referred to a foreigner who had set up production of carpets in Kashmir for export to Europe and India in the nineteenth century.

Based on a vague recollection I browsed through an old copy of the *Marg* where a reference to M/s Mitchell and Company is found, and where the company is credited with getting carpet manufacturing 'fairly well-established' in Kashmir already from the mid-nineteenth century. Thereby it also participated in ensuring a steady flow of Kashmir carpets to the West for the next five decades.[31] The company's existence is also verified by Sir Henry Watt who in his official catalogue for the Delhi Exhibition in 1903 wrote: 'The firm Mitchell & Co. sent only a few rugs, but these were very charming, perhaps the best woven and most artistically coloured of any Indian rugs at the exhibition.'[32] The latter quote refers to the time around which this carpet was produced. In 1915, the British explorer F. E. Younghusband, in his extensive description of Kashmir, also makes reference to Mitchell & Company and indicates that this business is thriving with among others exports to America.[33] While the pronunciation has become somewhat twisted and a company has become an

---
[31] *Marg*, p. 35.
[32] Sir George Watt: Official Catalogue, Delhi Exhibition 1903.
[33] Younghusband, p. 212.

individual in the course of time, there can hardly be any doubt that Mitchell and Company is the entity Mr Sayeed and his friends refer to in connection with this carpet.

As mentioned in the discussion of the previous carpet, there are good reasons to assume that the field of this carpet draws its inspiration from a similar field shown in the Vienna Catalogue. As in the case of the previous carpet, also the individual motif in this field is 'Indianized'. In this case, it includes presenting the predators in the short sides of the field as tigers rather than the original leopards. The field is given an off-white background colour—as in the original. Since this carpet is larger, the medallion comparative to the overall size of the carpet becomes slightly smaller. This creates more space for enlarging the individual elements and the space between them, and permits inclusion of a nearly continuous circle of cloud bans between the aura and the border. Cloud bands are originally a Chinese motif that depicts 'heavenly rest'.[34] No dragons are introduced, and all in all the design presents a more inviting field than the one in the Vienna Catalogue, and certainly more so than the previous interpretation. One gains a feeling that the designer has tried to create an impression of the sun shining down on a jungle of serenity—in spite of the significant existence of predators.

Without such a design, and my interpretation of what the field depicts, it would be difficult to see any connection between the field and the border. One could rather gain an impression that designer or a master artisan was forced by the client to design a carpet based on the client's wishes. Wishes that had developed after having come across a beautiful field and an extremely interesting set of borders, even if they were completely unconnected. This might sound surrealistic, but such demands were not uncommon in connection with carpets produced for export during the late nineteenth and the early twentieth century. A number of writers has lamented this kind of influence.[35]

Sir Birdwood claims to have raised this issue already in 1878 and certainly tears into his countrymen's lack of understanding in 1884. Forbes in 1866 warns of dire consequences if such practises are not abandoned. And Watts highlights the issue of European and American dictation with the following summing-up quote from local producers: 'This is the class of carpets we are compelled to manufacture. We would much rather turn out a better article, but we are in the hands of this person and at that who takes all our carpets".

The above, however, is very unlikely to have been the case of this particular carpet. Since it was found in North India in 2006, it is most likely produced by Mitchell & Company on a commission, along the lines described by Sir Birdwood. That is, where the client has indicated to the company

---
[34]Henry T. Harris, *Carpet Weaving Industry of Southern India*, Government Press, 1908, p. 58.
[35]Birdwood, *Industrial Arts of India*, 1884, p. 377.

and the designer where and how the carpet is planned to be used, the size, and the basic theme of interest, and left it to them to design and execute the carpet in their own time.[36]

In spite of the field being both detailed and beautiful, the space that merits the most attention is unquestionably the borders. Starting from the field is a narrow border depicting a continuous row of unsophisticated small flowers. The main border is quite wide, showing angels ('winged human-like creatures') standing side by side looking inward towards the field and covering all but the very central position of the longitudinal borders. Into those positions are inserted motifs showing a bird hovering over a low structure with a blue central area, the whole motif being lit up by rays of light coming from back and above. On each side of the boarder are smaller borders in with a row of alternately positioned simple crosses and palmettes.

The question it raises is, however, who or what kind of institution may have commissioned such a carpet.

Border detail

As mentioned on other occasions nearly all carpet weavers in Kashmir were, and are even today, Muslims. Angels or winged human-like creatures figure as part of the faith among both Muslims and Christians. They also figure in Indian mythology. Such creatures are often depicted in the corner of Persian carpets, and have found their way into carpets of Kashmiri designs.

---
[36]Birdwood, *Industrial Arts of India*, 1884, p. 374.

As mentioned in connection with the carpet shown on page xxx, crosses, however, are not motifs that are favoured in Islamic designs. Neither have I in other carpets of Kashmiri design encountered a motif such as the one centrally positioned in the main border of this carpet. This motif brings to mind the baptismal in Christian churches, and the dove descending on Christ during his baptism. The latter, is often found in glassworks or paintings in proximity to baptismal in churches, but the concept of baptism has no place in Islam. If the above is the correct interpretation of the motif, it seems inconceivable that a carpet with such a motif has should been commissioned by a Muslim.

As the Mitchell and Company was a European company and therefore would have no problems in designing and producing a carpet with such motifs as important elements in a carpet, a likely theory could be that the carpet was commissioned by a Christian, with the possible intention of donating this to decorate his/her church. If this should be the case, it would open a number of plausible interpretations of the picture painted in this work. This interpretation is supported by the fact that Mr Sayeed acquired the carpet from formally well-endowed Christian family. Until further research it will, however, remain just that—an interesting theory.

Medallion details

The Angel and Baptismal Carpet – Kashmiri
292 x 210 cm (9'7" x 6'11")

A CROSS CARPET FROM KASHMIR

Place of production: Kashmir
Year of production: Probably 1940s
Size: 173 x 119 cm (5'8" x 3'11")
Material: Wool on cotton warp and weft;
Knot: Senneh knots, 168/sq. inch woven in Jaipur back
Dye: Natural dyes

Given the typical structure of this carpet its origin from Kashmir has never been drawn into question. It is well made with good wool, good colour scheme, and is evenly worn. The carpet generally draws on motifs that are quite common in that region—such as the palmettes in the border; the basic shape of the field and the central medallion; the henna twigs and leaves—but nevertheless mange to create an uncommon total. A strong and clearly demarcated border, distinguishes it from many other Kashmiri designs. And, contrary to what is often the case, the field is lightly decorated. The most striking element, however, is the very central form which is difficult to describe as anything but a Coptic cross. By surrounding this cross with an open area of sun-yellow and thereafter the blue of the Feraghan shape gives the cross an impression of being lifted up from the rest of the field.

Coptic cross

Central motif in the Cross carpet

What a Coptic cross is doing in such a prominent position in a carpet, which was produced in Kashmir in late 1930s, or early 1940s, is an interesting question. A phrase borrowed from H. T. Harris in his discussion of the boteh seems appropriate: 'It is not to be supposed that the shape was chosen for such prominence without some real symbolic or religious reason.'

The Cross Carpet – Kashmiri
Probably second quarter of twentieth century
173 x119 (5'8" x 3'11")

The carpet is Kashmiri, and nearly without exception these carpets are designed and knotted by Muslims. As the carpet was found in India it was in all likelihood commissioned by an individual or institution that remained in India after Independence, otherwise it would have left the Indian shores a long time ago.

From literature it would be fair to say that mainstream Islam does have a rather ambiguous view on the issue of the cross and the crucifixion of Christ. The view generally expressed is that crucifixion is a most demeaning way of execution, and Allah would not have allowed Jesus, one of—if not the most prominent of his prophets prior to the Prophet Muhammad—to be killed in such a manner. With the above in mind, it is unlikely that a Muslim with such beliefs would have commissioned this carpet, or used such a motif in a carpet for his own use.

How dearly one would have liked to know for what purpose someone took the trouble of placing such a specific order; what thoughts the designer harboured in creating the design; as well as those of the weaver when implementing such an order. Unfortunately, this will remain an unfulfilled dream.

AN ARDABIL-INSPIRATION FROM KASHMIR

Place of production: Kashmir
Year of production: Probably second quarter of the twentieth century
Size: 173 cm x 119 cm (5'8" x 3'11")
Material: Wool on cotton warp and weft
Knot: Senneh knots, 168/sq. inch, woven in Jaipur back
Dye: Natural dyes

The design of the carpet has undoubtedly taken its inspiration from the famous Persian Ardabil carpet which for long has been displayed in the Victoria and Albert Museum.

This carpet was sold to me by a carpetwallah in Delhi—whose name I unfortunately do not remember. He claimed it was a carpet that had been used for a long time in a small mosque in Srinagar. This can well be a plausible tale given the fact that the carpet is quite worn, but evenly so—showing no signs of furniture marks or particularly worn-out paths which so often are apparent in carpets used in European style living rooms.

It is a nice and balanced, but a not spectacular carpet. It is well made in spite of a somewhat lower knot-count than what one associates with modern Kashmiri productions. Both the lower knot count as well as the subdued colours has in discussions with carpetwallahs been given as reasons for venturing the opinion that the carpet must have been produced on local commission, as well as for the probable period of production.

Ardabil Inspiration – Kashmiri Carpet
Second quarter twentieth century
173 x 119 cm (5'8" x 3'11")

THE PEACOCK CARPET, KASHMIR

Place of production: Kashmir
Year of production: Completed 1979
Size: 152 cm x 92 cm (5' x 3')
Material: Silk pile on cotton warp and weft.
Knot: Senneh knots, 676/sq. inch woven in Jaipur back.

We have stuck to this idea. Fortunately, my wife has a knack for balance and colours in interior decoration Already at the onset of our rather nomadic life my wife and I decided that we, rather than cluttering our home with a multitude of 'tourist' memorabilia of questionable quality, would concentrate our limited resources on a few items of value from each of the places we ended up living or visiting—items that would have practical/decorative use of in our home in Norway. The number of items and their individual value might have increased beyond what we originally had envisaged, and. She has therefore been able to blend these items rather elegantly together in our modest abode in Oslo, as well as other places in which we have resided. We acquired this carpet from Shaw brother's outlet at the Hotel Le Meridien in New Delhi in the early part of 1991 as a memento of our first posting in India. The purchase also signalled my serious efforts to learn more about Indian carpets.

According to the information provided by Shaw & Sons the carpet is one of a twin pair made in parallel from 1976 to 1979 by Ghulam Nabi Dauda. Dauda was from Srinagar and had been making carpets for forty years in the art and was regarded as one of the most skilled artisans of this period. The design was named moredar, which simply means peacocks. The carpets were acquired by Shaw & Sons, one at the time, in the period 1987–89. The twin was bought by a gentleman from Frankfurt some time in 1990. To their knowledge only these two carpets were made of this design. The last information was naturally of significance for any collector. Given the time that it must have been taken to create the design and prepare the talim the latter information, if correct, would be remarkable. I have consequently over the last twenty-five years—whenever going through piles of carpets—been on the lookout for 'copies'. Fortunately, so far without success.

Whether the piece is as unique as indicated or not, the design is certainly uncommon. It is also well-balanced, with a beautiful and appropriate combination of colours, and top-quality execution. If any criticism can be levelled at the design, it would be that the designer—in the same manner as with the 'millflower' creations—has crowded the field to an extent where very close scrutiny is required to capture its intricacies.

Surprisingly, given the workmanship that has gone into the carpet, it has a cotton warp and weft—not as one would assume—one made in its entirety of silk.

Central 'medallion' created by peacocks, neck to neck

Border detail

The Peacock Carpet – Kashmiri 1975–80
152 x 92 cm (5' x 2')

REGRETTED SALE

Place of production: Kashmir
Year of production: Around 1980
Size: 152 cm x 91 cm (5' x 3')
Material: Good wool on cotton warp and weft
Knot: Senneh knots, 400/square inch

Collecting carpets as a hobby means running into situations where you are presented with a carpet you would like to acquire, but lack the funds to do so. If this predicament happens in New Delhi and your carpetwallah is financially comfortable, he might be willing to take one of your carpets to cover the missing amount. I have sometimes accepted this option—in most cases to my later regret.

Such was the case with this carpet I originally found in a small shop in the Ashoka Hotel in New Delhi in 1991. Since the proprietor had been peddling the carpet for several years, I was able to acquire it for a reasonable price. When viewing the carpet, it is understandable that it had been difficult to sell. It obviously does not answer to the general expectation of his 'tourist clientele'.

The carpet has no traditional border. The field extends to the edge, but the outer part of the field is densely covered by a flower pattern that creates an illusion of a border. The central 'medallion' can seem to resemble the herati pattern, but it is a unique creation. The medallion draws attention to the centre, but also spread light to the rest of the central part. An unusual, interesting creation—if one is able to disengage from normal expectations of how a piled carpet should be designed.

Several authors have indicated that carpets designed and executed in Kashmir often are influenced by designs used in its famous shawl industry. In the late 1940s and early 1950s there were also conscious efforts to create more 'indigenous' carpet patterns based on shawl designs.[37] The idea, however, did not seem to catch the market. Still attempts have every now and then been made to revive the idea. This carpet must be regarded as a determined and successful effort to transmit the shawl pattern to a piled carpet. A similar effort is shown by E. Gans-Ruedin.[38] Whoever later bought this carpet from Mr Sayeed should count her/himself fortunate in finding an unusual, but worthy item.

---

[37] Chattopadhyay.
[38] E. Gans-Ruedin, *Indian Carpets*, p. 176.

A MODERN KASHMIRI DESIGN

Place of production: Kashmir
Year of production: 1985–90
Size: 183 cm x 122 cm (6' x 4')
Material: Silk pile on silk warp and weft;
Knot: Senneh knots, 484/sq. inch and woven in Jaipur back

Our intuition and 'hunch' can provide much to the process of decision-making provided they are applied in areas that are familiar to the decision-maker. In the early 1990s, I certainly was in unfamiliar territory when I bought this carpet in New Delhi—simply because I thought it looked interesting and would suit our living room. I must therefore confess that my luck was better than my knowledge.

There are carpets that are technically excellent, have a pleasing design, and even have colours that match the surrounding for which they are intended, but which you nevertheless forget no sooner you have walked over it. Then, there are carpets that might 'disturb' your senses at first encounter, but tend to 'grow' on you when it is revisited. This carpet fortunately proved to be in the latter category.

At first glance, this 'silk-on-silk' carpet gives an impression of being a carpet of the 'scrolling-vine-and-blossom pattern'.[39] The designer, however, decided to enclose the palmettes and flowers in the central part of the field with a marked border, and composing these elements on a white background. In one sense, this is disturbing as it induces a form of medallion into a scrolling-vine-and-blossom pattern. It further breaks with the tradition of such carpets from the Mughal period where the tendency was to present the field as one single composition—less it was with prayer carpets. The form, while being elegant and pleasing, is different from any other Indian medallion design I have encountered. For a Kashmiri design, the carpet also has an uncommonly strong border in which the designer has again accentuated individual elements by placing them on a white background.

Once the above deviations from tradition is recognized and accepted, the design presents the carpet as an elegant modernization of Kashmiri tradition, with balanced colour combinations and excellent technical execution. After twenty years with heavy traffic, it is no worse for wear.

---

[39]Walker, *Flowers Underfoot*.

5

Carpet from the Deccan and the South

INITIAL INTRODUCTION OF CARPETMAKING

As mentioned earlier a second, but less-known avenue of piled carpet introduction to the subcontinent seems to have taken place in the south-eastern part even before Akbar introduced his Persian weavers in the north. This took place in present-day state of Andhra Pradesh when four Persian weaver families landed and established their trade in Masulipatam in mid-fifteenth century.[1]

Not surprisingly, no early documents in English collaborating this event are identified. However, in a report from 1672 Sir Streynsham Master—an official of the East India Company—writes from his visit that 'this Elloru is reckoned one of the greatest Townes in this country (Golconda), where are made your best carpetts, after the manner of those in Persia, by a race of Persians which came over 100 years ago.' Moreover, Henry T. Harris, who visited Elluru at the turn of the nineteenth and twentieth centuries, concludes his discussion on the topic as follows 'We may assume with some reason that the industries in Elluru and Masulipatam actually date from about the middle of the fifteenth century.'[2] Finally in 1965, Jasleen Damija met with some of the weaver families in Elluru who were recognized as direct descendants of the four Persian families mentioned above. According to their tradition their forefathers landed in Masulipatam about 600 years ago. Some hundred year later descendants of three of these families moved to Elluru where plants used for dyeing grew wild.[3] Allowing a bit of leeway for verbal history this information corresponds well with that mentioned above.

The idea that Persian carpet weavers should have settled in this area already in the middle of the fifteenth century is not at all as far-fetched as one at first glance could believe. Apart from what is already mentioned one must take into account that Masulipatam on the Coromandel Coast was at this time the most important port on the eastern coast of India. In addition to Indians from a number of states, this harbour served Arab, Chinese, Portuguese, and Persian traders. Persian

---
[1]While one seems to accept the manner in which the introduction took place, flexibility must be exercised in determining the exact timing until such time that written documentation can be identified from the relevant period.
[2]Harris, *Carpet weaving Industry of Southern India*.
[3]Dhamija, *Marg*, p. 32b.

carpets would therefore not have been an unknown commodity, and most probably sought after. However, that a group of Persian weavers would have decided to travel from Persia to Masulipatam purely on basis of a possibility of securing a market for their trade seems highly unlikely. Such a voyage would even at the best of times have been precarious, the cost of such undertaking beyond the means of the weavers, and the difficulties associated with managing to settle into a strange land and culture daunting. It is more than probable therefore, that they would have had support, or a promise that patronage would be forthcoming. either from some of the Persian merchants trading on these shores, from an emissary of one of the Indian rulers, or a combination of the two. That the Bahmani sultanate had conquered Warangal in 1425 and thereby also gained control of the coast and Masulipatam makes the latter assumption most probable.

The Bahmanis descended from Turko–Persian nobility and is known to have been strong promoters of Persian language and culture. They would therefore likely have encouraged establishment of carpet production in their own domain.

It is also documented that the Qutb sultans and their noblemen who followed the Bahmanis as rulers of Golconda and Warangal from 1512, continued patronizing the arts, and are likely to have extended this also to the art of carpet-making.

Patronage, represented as important a financial backbone for production of quality carpets in the south as it did in the north. That such support must have been available can be deduced from studying the carpets that exists from this period. Similarly, from records of Dutch trade in carpets from the Deccan as early as 1666.[4] It is simply not conceivable that production of carpets of such sizes and quality have taken place and made available for export, without some form of patronage from the ruling elite.

The patronage would also have facilitated carpet-makers in moving from one base to another. Such patronage supports Damija's assumption that it was individuals or groups from the families in Elluru who also before 1650, established production in Warangal. Since Aurangzeb generally was no supporter of art, and no record of royal involvement in carpet production has been identified, Damija's theory seems more plausible than the folklore claim that carpet production first was introduced following Aurangzeb's conquest of the Deccan in 1667.[5]

---

[4]Walker, *Flowers Underfoot*, figures 119, 140, and p. 20; also *Sultans of the South*, figs. 17 and 21.
[5]Walker, *Flowers Underfoot*, p. 14.

THE NIZAM RULE

In the aftermath of Aurangzeb's death in 1707, the power of the Mughal empire gradually declined. In 1724, Mir Qamar-ud-din Khan was granted the title and authority of ashaf jah (grand vizier) of his domain. While retaining the title of nizam he became de facto hereditary ruler of the state of Hyderabad, and established himself with Hyderabad city as his capital.

Following the tradition of the former independent rulers on the Deccan, Asaf Jah—the first nizam—and his noblemen became active patrons of a Persian based culture. The first nizam died in 1748, but with exception of some turbulent thirteen years after his death, the practice of providing patronage seems to have continued for the next 200 years. It has left its mark on architecture, literature, music, dance, and cuisine, as well as in the designs and techniques of such decorative arts as textiles and piled carpet productions.

In addition to support from local rulers and their courts the production on the Deccan Plateau seems to have been able to respond positively to demands from foreign markets. A sizeable Dutch trade in carpets from the Deccan and the Coromandel Coast therefore started—as mentioned above—as early as in 1666, and continued to the end of the eighteenth century. There are also indications that the East India Company ordered some hundred numbers of carpets from Elluru in 1681. The British interest, however, does not seem to have been sustained for any duration

The export also included trade with carpets in Japan.[6] In his catalogue for the exhibition *Flowers Underfoot: Indian Carpets of the Mughal Era*, Daniel S. Walker depicts a number of astonishing carpets attributed to the Deccan from the period between mid-seventeenth to the early nineteenth century. Several of these carpets are found in Japanese museums and are documented to have arrived with Dutch traders operating from their trading post on Nagasaki. The Dutch also supplied their home markets in Europe. The production they were able to place their hands upon would have been small in comparison to what was produced for the rulers of the time under the patronage culture. There are therefore reasons to assume that the centres in Deccan during this period had a considerable production both in terms of quantity and quality.

The comparative advantage the Deccan plateau and surrounding areas had for carpet production was an altitude and climate conducive to sheep rearing. In addition to local wool South India had further already in the seventeenth century been recognized for production of excellent silk, and

---

[6]Ibid., p. 20.

some of the weaving centres were known for producing valuable carpets with silk pile.[7] It was also an advantage that a number of plants useful for dye production were growing wild on the plateau. As mentioned above the latter was apparently a strong reason for the Persian families relocating from Masulipatam to Elluru in the mid-sixteenth century.[8]

Availability of raw material, in-depth knowledge of dyeing techniques, trained designers and weavers combined with increased markets lead to expansion of the industry from Masulipatam, Elluru, and Warangal to other centres in the Deccan such as Bijapur, Hyderabad, and Golconda. Later, around 1750, it also spread to Mysore where information indicates that Haidar Ali (1722–82) established carpet production with weavers he got from Golconda, Bijapur, and North India.[9] The production of silk carpets in Ayampet also seems to have started around this time.

Towards the end of the eighteenth century, carpet production waned in the South as it did in the North. This was not due to lack of skilled carpetmakers. Rather it was a result of reduced demand domestically—were a new breed of elite found themselves better served by imported status symbols. The nizam's domain, however, seems to have been an exception. At the same time foreign demands dropped due to turbulent economic times in Europe.

Also, the general artistic quality of the production might have fallen during the early part of the nineteenth century. Carpets of excellence from Elluru, Warangal, and Hyderabad, and possibly also from other centres in the South, must, however, have continued to be made on a limited scale. Such carpets were exhibited at the Great Exhibition of 1851, contributing in no small measure to the rediscovery of Indian carpets in the European and American markets.

From the late 1850s, the interest created by the London Exhibition led to a growth in existing, and establishment of new carpet producing centres in the South. Available documentation shows that more than twenty carpet centres were in active in the South between 1855 and the turn of the twentieth century.[10] At several of these centres, silk—of which there was an excellent production—became the preferred material for the pile.

However, in contrast to exports in the seventeenth and eighteenth centuries this time the larger market was created by the craving of the many with restricted means, rather than that of the few who could afford and craved for quality and exclusivity. T. N. Mukharji might have hit the nail on

---

[7] Walker, *Flowers Underfoot*, p. 147.
[8] *Marg*, p. 32a.
[9] Harris, *Monograph*, p. 5.
[10] Birdwood, Mukharji, Forbes Watson, Watt, Thurston and Harris.

the head already in 1888 when he in the introduction to Indian carpets presented at the Glasgow International Exhibition wrote: 'The public is now the patrons of arts and the public can only afford to have the name, not the reality. So things for the most part are now getting made and sold not always for any intrinsic merit in them, but in virtue of their traditional reputation.'[11]

Gone were most of the patronage of the rulers and their retinue. This patronage could certainly be demanding, but the patrons were able to communicate in understandable terms what was expected and what was not. They also represented customers who were at hand to express their dissatisfaction to those that produced the carpets, but also to reward a piece of art well done. And they could as no other provide the artists and artisans recognition beyond mere material wealth. These were all elements of a culture that proved so well suited for production of excellence in what were both a demanding craft as well as an art.

Initially the surge in export demand undoubtedly was a blessing for the weavers. It created much needed means of survival in a culture which left little room for changing means of livelihood. As in the north of the subcontinent as well as in Iran[12] such export driven increase, however, also brought with it the commercial imperative of the European and American markets. Indian carpetmakers were suddenly faced with adapting to a culture of commerce which both they and their rulers proved ill equipped to handle.

The Indian carpetmaker's production was no longer dictated by knowledge and traditions built up over centuries. What now dominated production were such concerns as delivery schedules and perceived market demands, and patterns and colours formed in a physical, cultural and religious reality far from those producing the products. Further, the southern producers in particular had to cope with a demand 'that required the products to be cheap, above everything else'.[13] This naturally, but unfortunately, lead to use of shoddy and unsuitable material for warp, weft, and pile, and shoddy workmanship in the products made for export. Of even more significance and far-reaching consequence was the introduction of aniline dyes, an experiment that was relatively short-lived, but long enough to make significant damage to the market for many of the centres in the South. Into this was also brought the competition from carpet production in the jails.[14]

H. T. Harris also points out that the Southern carpetmakers had to deal with a serious challenge

---

[11] Mukharji, *Art-Manufactures of India*.
[12] Roy, p. 202.
[13] Roy, p. 203.
[14] See chapter on Jail Carpets.

the northern units avoided—lack of quality wool.¹⁵ As mentioned earlier, one of the reasons for the establishment of a carpet production on the Deccan was availability of acceptable wool. Production of wool in the Deccan was, however, never large because sheep rearing concentrated on meat production rather than wool. When the industry now faced heavy demand they was forced to use chunnam wool to meet the prize demand of their new customers.

The results of these regrettable developments are already touched upon in the introductory chapter on subcontinental carpets production in general.¹⁶

While the surge of interest stemming from the 1851 exhibition was felt all over the subcontinent there are indications that the negative effects became more pronounced and consequently more damaging to the carpet industry in the South—this in spite of having carpet centres with as long, and in some ways even more unique and strong tradition than those in the North. A plausible explanation for this might be found in the following:

To an even greater extent than in the North the general climate in the South limited the natural market for piled carpet; the jail production will have undercut prices in the local 'bread and butter' segment; and no efforts seems to have been made on part of those who financed the industry to identify markets in other parts of India. This situation reduced the local market to a small elite. With few exceptions, this was an elite that by this time tended to prefer inferior foreign status symbols to the real products¹⁷.

Most of the writers who wrote on the subject during the latter part of the nineteenth and early twentieth centuries lamented the reduction in the traditional patronage role of the elite, a development which seemed to have been ongoing at a gradually increasing speed from the latter part of the eighteenth century. They recognized the strength of the patronage system in maintaining a small but high-quality production with artistic merit and value. At the same time, they lamented its rapid replacement by Western capitalistic production-imperative, and introduction of carpet production in the jails.

These factors are likely to have increased the lure of any export market and limited the industries bargaining power opposite foreign buyers and their demands for change in design, quality, as well as prices. An additional element increasing their vulnerability might have been that a very small community of Muslim immigrants ran carpetmaking in the Deccan. In the very traditional Hindu majority these weavers would—with very few alternatives of livelihood—have been unable to put

---

¹⁵Harris.
¹⁶See chapter on Indian Carpets.
¹⁷Harris, *Monograph*, p. 11. It should, however, be noted that both the maharaja of Mysore and later the nizam of Hyderabad during the same period opted to use local productions for their new palaces.

up a fight against the export markets exploitation.

However, a report from the Madras Exhibition in 1857 indicates that carpet production in South India still maintained their standards. The report from the juries at the exhibition describes carpets from Tanjore (Aijampet), Ellore, North Arcot, Hyderabad including Warangal, Mysore and Bangalore. With few exceptions these carpets received commendation from good to decidedly excellent. Nevertheless, it is worth noting that the comments of a woollen carpet from Tanjore conclude 'the design with exception of the border is an imitation of a bad English manufacture'.[18]

In the following decades several writers of repute warned of the consequences of letting what can only be described as a raw and short-sighted capitalism to continue unrestricted. Unfortunately, this had little effect, and the review carried out by H. T. Harris in 1908 shows an alarming situation with five or six centres having ceased to exist or in the process of doing so. This included the famous production in Masulipatam and Ayyampet. Ayyampet had been known for interesting design and good workmanship—particularly in silk pile. Here the number of families involved in production had dropped from 107 to 12 between 1875 and 1885, and in 1906 it was recorded that the cheaper jail-made woollen rugs have destroyed the industry there, woollen carpets are rarely made, and silk ones never, except on order.[19] Even at the well-known centre in Elluru—which still had a sizable production—the quality had become outright poor in all respects.

The above apparent degradation of production was, however, according to the writers not due to lack of knowledge or skills on part of those producing the carpets, but simply due to lack of middlemen and markets that could appreciation carpetmaking as an art, and that excellence in production had its price. From the above one should therefore not draw the conclusion that no carpets of value were produced in this region during the latter part of the nineteenth century. Interestingly it was typically the export articles that represented degradation of design, colours, and workmanship—not production for the local market.[20]

The view of the carpets that were produced on explicit orders in Ayampet in 1906 was for instance that they 'are excellent in quality, especially the latter (silk), but the colour combination are not always pleasing'.[21] The same applied to carpets made on order for the local market in Elluru".[22]

---

[18]Edward Balfoure, Madras Exhibition of Raw Products, Arts, and Manufactures of Southern India: Report of the Juries, 1858, p. 149.
[19]*Tanjore District Gazetteer*, 1906.
[20]Sir George Watt, Official Catalogue – Delhi Exhibition 1903, pp. 427–228 and 439; Harris, *Monograph*, p. 53.
[21]Ibid.
[22]Harris, *Monograph*, p. 13.

At Warangal, which had a thriving industry and received praise as late as at the Delhi Exhibition in 1902, experiments with aniline dyes. This resulted during the next decade in serious setbacks. But as in the case of Elluru quality carpets continued to be made when such were ordered. In addition it is recorded that quality carpets continued to come from the nizam's court workshop in Hyderabad, and units in Golconda, Hamakunda and Gulbarg—where the local elite were likely to have followed the nizam's example and strengthened the local market by maintaining an interest in quality carpets. The Salarjung Museum in Hyderabad has a collection of carpets from this period, some of which have been identified as coming from court workshops.

In addition, came the prison units whose state patronage undoubtedly led to the closure of many private units in the South, but they produced some excellent carpets. Records indicate that piled carpet production took place at some ten jails in the South. Of these Vellore and Bangalore Central Prisons were particularly commended for a considerable production of well executed carpets of good design and colouring. (This was the case even if the Bangalore prison at the time of T. H. Harris's report had used some aniline colours. Fortunately the practice was quickly discarded). The production at both prisons is interestingly documented to have been established with assistance of carpet makers from Elloru, probably in the 1860s.

Today samples of such quality carpets can be found through a targeted search in India itself, since what was exported were produced for a market that neither had understanding of quality, nor the means to afford a quality that could have been provided.

Little documentation seems so far to have been unearthed which could throw light on developments in southern piled carpet production in the fifty years from 1910 to mid-1960s. I have, however, in the case of Warangal come across documentation that shows that their production—after a disastrous experiment with aniline dyes and subsequent patronage by the state of Hyderabad—got back to production of superior quality carpets. The nizam proved an important patron of this effort when he contracted the entire carpet requirements for his new palace in Delhi—Hyderabad House—to this unit. The production of this unit was gradually supplemented with mass production of cheaper products aimed at the local middle classes. However, this production continued up to inclusion of Hyderabad state in the Indian union.[23]

In 1965 a reputed Indian art magazine produced a copy which gives commendable—though sketchy—descriptions of the industry in Elluru and Warangal. These were apparently the only

---

[23] V. Ramakrishna Reddy: Economic History of Hyderabad State, p. 500.

surviving centres in the South at that time, but shows that carpetmakers in these places continued some production in spite of poor conditions. In Elluru there were around 650 weavers of whom some 600 worked for six different private companies producing extremely poor-quality carpets for export to UK. The remaining produced traditional designs of better-quality carpets as members of a cooperative society.

In the formally well-known centre of Warangal—where in the first quarter of the twentieth century more than 500 weavers were at work—only forty looms remained in operation. Here the traditional designs were followed, but also in this case of very poor quality. A gloomy picture indeed.

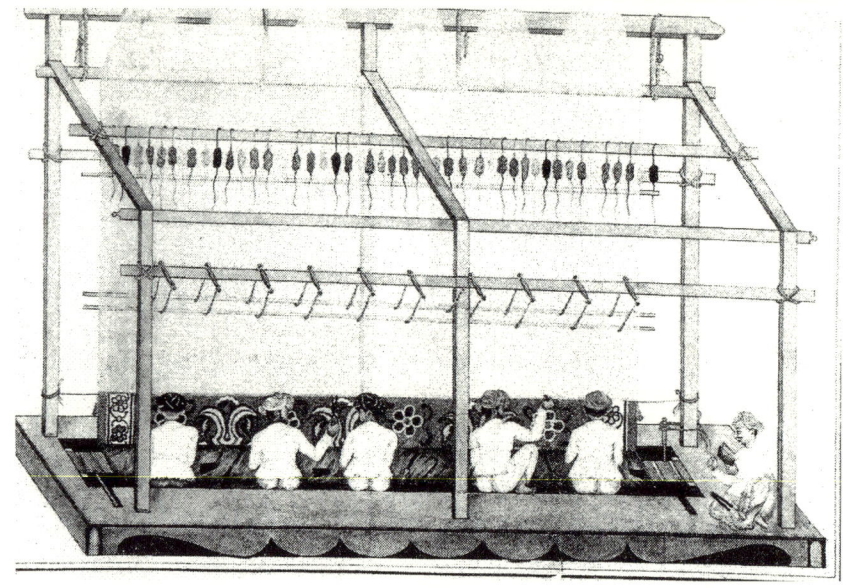

Carpet Production in the South

But old habits and skills die hard in India, and when attempting to identify the present situation one finds that there is again a thriving carpet industry in Elluru, Warangal, and Vellore. This includes handmade piled carpets of various designs—some of which obviously takes inspiration from traditional designs from the area. The carpets are produced on order and for the export market. They are marketed as being in the inexpensive range with a low knot count, but good quality wool. However, finer silk carpets are also made. Given that old techniques are still in use for these productions, one can assume that also higher grades of carpets can be produced on demand.

TRADITIONAL TRELLIS PATTERN FROM ELLURU

Place of production: Probably Elluru or Warangal
Year of production: Probably early twentieth century
Size: 220 cm x 147 cm (7'3" x 4'10")
Material: Wool on stout cotton warp and weft.
Knots: Senneh knot 49/sq. inch with depressed warp
Dye: Natural dyes

ABOUT CARPET PRODUCTION IN ELLURU

The carpetwallah who sold me this carpet in 1993 readily admitted that he did not know where it was produced. He was, however, quite sure that it did not come from any of the well-known production centres in North India.

After discussions with other carpetwallahs and with reference to literature, there are strong reasons to believe that it probably originates from Elluru. It can, however also have been made in Warangal.

As mentioned in the introduction to this chapter the weavers in Elluru trace their ancestors back to five Persian weaver families who likely arrived in Masulipatam in the mid-fifteenth century. Some hundred years later, four of the five families moved to Elluru, probably because of easier access to wool and plants required for making dyes. In 1672, the industry in Elluru—which at that time was a significant town—is reported to be thriving and meeting both local and export demands. Particularly the Dutch merchants seem to have been active in this trade from 1766, and for the next hundred years. There are reasons to believe that the industry in Elluru maintained a production even through the difficult period in the latter part of the eighteenth century.

The revival of interest in carpets from the Indian subcontinent following the Great Exhibition also benefitted Elluru. Dr Forbes writes, 'The rugs from Elluru were universally admired for their great characteristics of beautiful Oriental pattern, fine weave, and rich colouring, these seem well adapted to find ready sale in Europe.' Moreover, at the Madras Exhibition in 1857 carpets exhibited by S.

Nummiah received excellent commendation.[24] Consequently, a demand for these carpets bloomed—particularly in the UK. As late as 1880, Sir George Birdwood stated 'these, which are known in the London market by the name of Coconada, the place of their shipment on the Coromandel Coast, prove that carpets of uncontaminated native design and integrity of quality are still made by weavers of India, but of varieties not yet generally recognized by huckstering European dealers.... They are equal to anything ever produced in the Deccan'. These statements were naturally beneficial during its initial phases. However, as described earlier the pressure of the export market led to a corruption of precisely the rich heritage that made these carpets interesting.

By early twentieth century the export production from Elluru no longer stood up to any scrutiny—except to the bottom level of the commercial export market.[25] The industry did, however, still employed about 3,000 weavers on some 400 looms, and when weavers occasionally made carpets on order for local and foreign dignitaries and 'if the men are left to themselves and are not too much restricted in the matter of price, they are capable of producing carpets and rugs of as good quality as ever they did'.[26] The weavers still had excellent old patterns and good carpets were therefore produced in limited numbers also in the coming years, but the old skills of dyeing and execution were apparently fast disappearing.

But hereditary weavers had few if any alternatives of livelihood and in spite of limited market opportunities a dwindling group of weavers kept producing carpets for whatever markets they could find. Between H. T. Harris's report from 1908, and a brief review in 1965, it has so far not been identified documentation of the carpet industry in Elluru.[27] In the latter it is documented that poor quality carpets continued to be produced for export to the UK. Production took place under very poor working conditions. Weavers connected to the local weavers cooperative purchase and sales society were, however, producing better quality carpets with traditional design.

Today, more than fifty years later, production has yet again picked up on the basis of demand in foreign markets. Elluru has again been included among carpet-producing centres in India. Inexpensive rugs and carpets made on order dominate the production—many do, however, including elements of the traditional patters of the area.

---

[24] Balfoure, *Madras Exhibition*, p. 149.
[25] Harris, *Monograph*, p. 6.
[26] Ibid., p. 12.
[27] Dhamija, *Marg*.

ABOUT THE CARPET

The carpet in question probably dates from the early twentieth century, and belongs to those mentioned above as having been especially ordered by some local dignitary.

The trellis pattern applied in the field is a pattern traditionally employed by the weavers in Elluru, and closely resembles those that went under the local name of Reddy Khani (Reddy being the name of a significant benefactor and Khani being the term used for the design of the field). The border, however, shows a greater resemblance to those found in some of the carpets from Warangal.

The knot count is low, but by using stout cotton warp and weft combined with the technique of depressed warp the carpet gives a solid impression. The colours are pleasing. Undoubtedly, they originally were sharper, but have mellowed well. The patters are surprisingly rich considering the low knot count. It would therefore be fair to claim that the carpet amply demonstrates what learned carpet appreciators keep repeating: 'That the knot count is not all that gives a carpet artistic and commercial value. It is the manner in which the material, colours and the technical aspects are combined in order to carry a pleasing design that gives it value.'

The carpet has obviously been appreciated by generations of owners since it bears the mark of numerous repairs over different periods—none of them of any great excellence. This is particularly the case of areas coloured in the 'mid dark blue' and dark brown colours. The pile in these areas have also been the subject of 'oxidation erosion', and been attempted repaired without replacements matching the original natural dyes. This, of course, makes the carpet of less interest to anyone collecting carpets as an investment. For me its merits were to be found in the design and the manner in which it was constructed. Given that it was offered for a reasonable prize, it has been an interesting and pleasing acquisition from an area from where I had no other specimen.

Border detail

A trellis pattern, probably from Elluru
Early twentieth century

A CARPET FROM WARANGAL

Place of production: Probably Warangal, Hyderabad
Year of production: Likely mid-1930s
Size: 193 cm x 125 cm (6'4" x 4'1")
Material: Wool on stout cotton warp and a blue cotton weft
Knots: Senneh knot 100/sq. inch with depressed warp
Dye: Natural dyes

ABOUT WARANGAL

Warangal was established as the capital of the Kakatiya dynasty from the twelfth to the fourteenth centuries. The dynasty left tangible evidence of their rule in form of fortress and monuments. The entire centre of the old city centre was actually carved out of a rock and is a place to visit even if the city no longer has an elevated status. In 1425 the area fell to the Bahmanid Sultanate who then controlled an area from the west to the east coast of the Sub-Continent. The Bahamians descended from Persian nobility and is known to have been strong promoters of Persian language and culture. This royal patronage continued with the Qutb Shahi dynasty that ruled Golconda of which Warangal was a part from 1518 to 1687. It later continued under the rule of the nizams of Hyderabad from 1724 to 1948. With an interlude of some twenty years under Aurangzeb, people in Warangal continued to associate with, uphold and develop their Persian heritage. Competence in literature, painting, and other cultural expressions were held in high esteem and received patronage by the elite over a period of more than five centuries. Also the art and crafts of carpet making received such benefits from around the mid-fifteenth century.

CARPET PRODUCTION IN WARANGAL

Over the centuries, centres in the former state of Hyderabad in general, and at Warangal in particular, have provided carpets of great beauty and accomplishment. It is therefore regrettable that with exception of J. Cohen no researcher or student of art have found it interesting enough to make its history and accomplishment subject for a serious study. This is particularly so as there are good reasons to assume that research of Persian and Urdu material in the museums of Hyderabad and in the nizam's archives is likely to yield good results of such endeavour.

Lacking the above, I have attempted to stitch together a short overview from material that are available in English and might give a general understanding and help to those inclined to take on the above challenge.

As mentioned earlier the initial carpet production in Warangal was probably established by descendants of the Persian weaver families which originally landed in Masulipatam in the mid-fifteenth century. According to family history four of the five families had moved to Elluru by the mid-sixteenth century in order to benefit from plants that were ideal for production of dyes, possibly also to come closer to the wool producing areas. Even if weavers in Warangal claim that carpet production in this area started after the area was reconquered by the Mughal empire in 1687, there are reasons to assume that, its introduction originally came from the South rather than the North.

In spite of lack of interest in and encouragement to the arts during the reign of Aurangzeb, increased communication would have provided opportunities for cultural cross-fertilization between the North and the South at Warangal. This in a layman's eyes seems evident when viewing some of the eighteenth-century carpets attributed to Warangal in the exhibition 'Flowers Underfoot'—even if the Deccan carpets continued to be made with a slightly different structure, relatively low knot count, and with the typical colour combinations associate with productions from that region.[28]

Carpet production in Warangal continued over the next centuries. From such carpets as mentioned above, and those exhibited at the Great Exhibition in London in 1851 one must assume that their ability to produce excellent works of art was maintained even if it only was on a reduced scale. Of the Warangal carpets exhibited at the Great Exhibition Sir George Birdwood states 'the very finest rugs exhibited were from Warangal, about eighty miles east of Hyderabad'.

While carpets from this long period reached Europe and even Japan, there are no documentation supporting an extensive export from Warangal—or Hyderabad—prior to mid-nineteenth century. One can therefore assume that the arts and crafts associated with making of carpets have been kept alive through patronage of the nizams and their noblemen. Documented evidence of the various nizams interest in and support to art generally supports this assumption. Likewise, it can be assumed that their interest also would have influenced their court and the elite generally.

---

[28] Walker, *Flowers Underfoot*.

The export market that opened up with the Great Exhibition was also gradually exploited by the state of Hyderabad. Commercial houses organized production through private loom owners in such places as Hyderabad City, Gulbarga, and Golconda, in addition to Warangal and its surrounding areas. Much of this production would have been made for export and therefore been of commercial quality. It is, however, also documented that part of the production in this period were high quality carpets produced for local noblemen and princely houses of Hyderabad and else were on the subcontinent.[29]

Silk and woollen piled carpets from Hyderabad were also shown at the Madras Exhibition in 1857. Several of these carpets received good reviews. Since no mention is made of the nizam's involvement—which normally would have been the case if they had official blessing—one must assume that these specimens came from commercial units rather than representing those produced under the nizam's patronage. However, the best of the woollen carpets exhibited was identified as being produced in Warangal.[30]

In 1866, Watson specifically commends a beautiful carpet produced in Warangal, and also shows sketches of this design he felt would be suitable for further production.[31] Thereafter carpets from Warangal and its surrounding areas appeared in a number of international exhibitions, generally receiving positive reviews. At the prestigious Indian Exhibition in Delhi in 1902 Warangal products—provided by both the nizam and the maharaja of Tripura—received commendation.[32]

The Warangal carpets remained popular up to the beginning of the twentieth century with considerable export both to UK and other parts of India.

Introduction of aniline dyes in production of carpets for export did, however, result in a dramatic setback for the industry in Warangal as well as other centres on the Deccan. The first documented reaction to this disastrous practice I have come across is a report from the Colonial and Indian Exhibition in London. After general positive comments on jail productions, the writer states, 'the free weavers of Warangal (as opposed to those in jails) spoils the excellent patterns and weaving by aniline dyes.'[33] Possibly, because the nizam was not properly informed Hyderabad did not follow the example of Kashmir and banned import of aniline dyes.

---

[29]Dhamija, *Marg*, p. 32b.
[30]Balfour, *Madras Exhibition*, p. 149.
[31]J. Forbes Watson, *Textile Manufactures and the Costumes of the People of India*, 1866, p. 143.
[32]Watt, Indian Arts Exhibition, p. 441.
[33]Colonial and Indian Exhibition, London 1886, official catalogue.

In addition, the Gazetteer of India from 1909 mentions the aniline disaster in the carpet industry. However, the same gazetteer also informs that 'woollen carpets of excellent make' (now) were turned out from Warangal and surrounding areas, in which a large trade was carried out with Europe. This might be an indication that the aniline mistake by then had been rectified in the case of Warangal.

Probably a combination of a fall in the European market; local preferences for foreign industrial products; the general economic trends moving investors and entrepreneurs to more modern and lucrative ventures; and the lack of state patronage, ran carpetmaking in Warangal into renewed difficulties in the latter part of the 1920s. From having around 350 looms and 225 families engaged in the trade in 1925 the industry rapidly dwindled, and in 1930 only 90 looms operated by 22 families remained active.

With the aim of restoring this decaying industry the Hyderabad government—most likely on the instigation of the nizam who looked at the outlying areas as his particular responsibility—decided to establish a government-financed experimental carpet factory at Warangal in 1929. There are indications that the well-known carpet entrepreneur Stavradies was engaged in this venture as consultant.[34]

The basic idea was to provide the youngsters from traditional weaver families with employment in production of superior quality carpets, and at the same time assist existing local weavers in production and marketing of their cheaper carpets and dhurries. In spite of active promotion by local dignitaries the traditional carpet makers were initially reluctant to join the establishment. The factory therefore had to admit 'non-professional' boys and train them at the factory. Only after four years of operation did the traditional weaver's attitude to the venture started changing.

From the early 1930s and until 1937 the factory concentrated its production on 'superior-quality carpets'. As planned the income from this production was combined with commissions from sale of a substantial numbers of cheap quality carpets produced by cottage weavers. These products were sold by the Cottage Industry Sales Depot in Hyderabad, or exported to the UK. In 1935, the factory was aided by large order of superior quality carpets placed by the nizam for his new palace in New Delhi. Later the factory also started producing some medium and cheap products that must have competed with the cottage industry.

The production in the 1930s was relatively stable. During the war years, the factory greatly benefited from the import war restrictions in the UK and closure of the Mediterranean route. This led to a

---

[34]Dhamija, *Marg*, p. 32c.

phenomenally increase in production of all quality variations. Unfortunately, the factory was unable to adjust to changing situations after the war and was closed down in 1946. In his analysis in 1987, V. Ramakrishna Reddy attributes its demise primarily to its inability to provide its weavers with an adequate income. The experiment therefore was unable to attain its original goal of revitalizing this well-recognized industry to its former prosperity and excellence.[35] The carpet production in Warangal thereafter continued its decay and by 1965, when the art historian Jasleen Dhamija made her survey little remained of a proud craft which by all likelihood dated back some five centuries.

I have not found any documentation throwing light on the plight of the carpet industry in Warangal in the last part of the twentieth century but one must assume that various small and cottage industry initiatives of the Andhra Pradesh government kept a rudimentary production going. Therefore, when the general demand for Indian carpets of all makes and shades surfaced in the new century it was possible to revitalize the handmade Warangal production. As in Elluru, carpets of all sort of design are produced on specific orders, and many still include traditional elements in their designs. Probably due to cost implication the majority maintain a relatively low knot count and are marketed as reasonably priced products.

A corner detail

---

[35]V. Ramakrishna Reddy, *Economic History of Hyderabad State (Warangal Suba 1911-1950)*, Delhi: Gyan Publishing House, 1987, p. 490.

Probably Warangal Carpet
Second quarter twentieth century
220 x 147 cm (6'4" x 4')

ABOUT THE CARPET

As in the case of the former carpet, the carpetwallah who sold me this carpet was unsure of its origin. The design as a whole do not—at first glance—match any of the known carpet producing areas. Border elements, the angular vines, and the style of the flowers they connect, however, can indicate a connection with Hyderabad or Warangal on the Deccan Plateau. The low knot count, but stout depressed cotton warp giving a more solid impression than the low knot count should indicate, strengthen this assumption. A good, but slightly coarse wool, the colour scheme with several shades of beige, pale green, and use of plain natural wool for the off-white areas, pulls in the same direction. This is a view shared by my carpetwallah.

The carpet does not represent the best of Warangal production. Such carpets are found in European and Japanese museums, or among private collectors in India and around the world. However, it is an interesting carpet. It was given my eldest daughter and her would-be-husband when they were engaged. It has now served them well as an ornament and as a space for my grandchildren to play in their early years. As a consequence, it has naturally become even more worn than when it was bought some twenty years ago. My daughter treats it as memorabilia—as some carpets should be—and plan finding a wall on which it can gracefully retire.

HYDERABAD AND CARPET PRODUCTION

HYDERABAD CITY AND ITS CARPET PRODUCTION

Hyderabad city with its history, architecture, literature, museums, cuisine, jewellery, textiles, and its mixture of ethnicities—and quite apart from its importance as one of the rapidly growing centres of the Indian knowledge industry—can in no way be given a fair presentation in a publication that primarily deals with piled carpets. I will therefore have to restrain myself to matters that can be judged as relevant to the main topic.

I will, however, as strongly as possible, recommend any visitor to the Indian subcontinent to place this city and its surroundings on their itinerary. It will certainly not be a waste of time.

Hyderabad city was established by Mohammed Quli Qutb Shah when a dramatic plague in the latter part of the sixteen century demonstrated that the fort city of Golconda no longer could accommodate a growing population safely. Virgin forestland was therefore identified some 8 kilometres to the east, the city of Hyderabad was planned, and construction started in 1591. Over the following six decades, the Qutb sultans developed Hyderabad economically and culturally, and the city and state became one of the great markets for diamonds, pearls, steel, arms, but also fabrics.

When Aurungzeb became the emperor, he found the independence of the Deccan sultanates to be a danger to the empire. After having consolidated his power in Delhi, he consequently embarked on a military campaign to bring the Deccan area under his domain. After several attempts, Aurungzeb succeeded in overrunning Golconda Fort in 1687, and replaced the reigning sultan with one of his governors. During the following decades, Hyderabad experienced a decline, but continued to be the significant city on the Deccan.

With the death of Aurangzeb in 1707, the Mughal empire lost much of its power, and the local governors gradually gained more autonomy. In 1724, Mir Qamar-ud-din Khan—who earlier had been granted the title of Nizam-ul-Mulk (regulator of the realm)—defeated the former governor who opposed his appointment. In turn, the emperor granted him the title and authorities of Ashaf Jah (grand vizier) of his domain. This made him the de facto hereditary ruler of the state of Hyderabad—and established him with Hyderabad as his capital. He, however, retained his nizam title. Both he and his successors also—at least nominally—kept the state of Hyderabad a dominion of the empire until the emperor in Delhi was dethroned by the British in 1858.

With exception of a short period after the death of the first Nizam, and in spite of gradually having to part with its territories on the coast to the French and British interests, Hyderabad continued its development under the nizam's rule up to the time it was integrated into the Indian union in 1948. This development can undoubtedly be accredited to peaceful succession and the gradual effect of the Peace Britannica. However, also to prudent governance. At times, this was as much due to wise hereditary Prime Ministers as to the Nizams themselves. The last four Nizams were, however, regarded as progressive rulers of their times.

As a result, the State of Hyderabad at the time of its integration into the Union of India covered an area of some two hundred and fifty thousand square-kilometre - close to the size of England, Welch and Scotland combined - and had a population of some 17 million. The State of Hyderabad had a developed governmental structure. It had its own judiciary, police, army, coinage, postal service, educational system, railway, roads and irrigation infrastructure. A university was founded, colleges established, and primary education was made compulsory and free for the poor. Also, its health system was gradually developed.

It is interesting to note that the army in addition to 5500 "native" troops also employed 3000 European and Arab mercenaries, and that several of the key administrators were foreigners hired by the state, not imposed by British India. Its economy – even though underdeveloped – was strong, and in spite of many of his predecessors being considerable spendthrifts, the Nizam was described as the world's richest individual.

The Nizams and many of their noblemen continued from the very inception the tradition of the Brahimi and Qutb rulers before them to encourage Persian based culture. They extended support to literature in Persian and Decani Urdu, and strengthened educational institutions. Their patronage covered such arts as miniature painting, music, dance, and certainly the development of a remarkable cuisine and etiquette. As their forerunners, they had great interest in architecture. Not the least the two last Nizams did much to place their mark on the architecture of the city with construction of astonishing buildings for the City Hospital, High Court, Library, Town Hall, Museum and Observatory. All are buildings that even today give Hyderabad its distinctive character.

As mentioned in previous chapters there had – with a basis in the patronage culture discussed above - been a considerable production of carpets of excellence from centres that at one time were part of the "State of Hyderabad". The better known of these were Masulipatnam, Elloru, and Warangal, but it also included the city of Hyderabad and nearby Golconda. From existing literature, there are reasons to believe that the Nizam maintained court workshops in both Hyderabad and Golconda. In the latter, there are indications that the production also included carpets with silk pile.

Documentation in English from these centres is, however, scanty. One probable reason can be that the State of Hyderabad seems to have enjoyed a greater internal autonomy than what was the case with other princely states on the Deccan. There was therefore less reason for officers of British India to carry out surveys or write reports on issues relating to production and commerce in this state. They might even not have been welcome. An indication of this is that the State of Hyderabad hardly received attention in the Imperial Gazetteer of India published in 1988. It was only when the 'State Gazetteers' was introduced in 1909 that Hyderabad received a more appropriate attention. That English documentation is limited do, however, not imply that no documentation exists. Traditionally both the Nizam's Royal Household and the State of Hyderabad maintained extensive accounts, stock ledgers, and similar information in Farsi and Urdu. A proper search in the museums, libraries, and private collections in Hyderabad is likely to bring forth significant and interesting information on the piled carpet production in this amazing city.

A NORWEGIAN OFFICER'S PURCHASE - THE SMISETH CARPET

Place of production: Probably the nizam's workshop, Hyderabad
Year of production: Between 1875 and 1880
Size: 580 cm x 354 cm (19'x11'7")
Material: Wool on cotton warp and cotton and wool weft.
Knots: Senna knot, varying between 80 and 100 knots/sq. inch
Dye: Vegetable dyes.

My youngest daughter, an intelligent, level-headed and independent young woman met her husband as a classmate at the tender age of fifteen. Part of the mutual attraction might have been that the boy's great-grandmother, Aimèe Sommerfelt, had written the well-known book *The Road to Agra* and my daughter had just returned from three years in Delhi and numerous visits to the famous monument—the Taj Mahal. Since neither my wife and I, or the young man's parents thought this youthful infatuation was likely to last, none of us took steps to build a relationship during the first couple of years. The relationship, however, lasted and we started visiting each other.

In the course of a conversation in their sizable library, I happened to mention that piled carpets was a particular hobby of mine. Doctor Smiseth then explained that the room we were sitting in had been the library of his wife's grandfather—Professor Alf Sommerfelt. Apart from housing a considerable collection of books and documents, which later was donated to the University of Oslo, the room also contained a very large piled oriental carpet. The carpet had been in the library since the early 1930s and had gradually become worse for wear. Not so long ago they had therefore found it necessary to role it up and stow it into the attic—not quite knowing what to do with it.

In my immediate estimate, the carpet had to be nearly 20' x 20' and not less than seventy years old, and the I naturally became interested. From looking at a photo of the carpet, it seemed most unlikely that it could be a Persian, Turkish, or even a standard North Indian carpet.

However, how could a possibly South Indian carpet of that size and age end up in a private home in Norway?

As Ms Smiseth was aware that various family tales surrounded the carpet, she decided to consult her more than eighty-year-old mother. Gradually the following information surfaced.

Ms Smiseth's great-great-grandfather—Mr Fredrik Gjertsen—apparently acquired this carpet from an officer who had served in British India. This happened sometime after Mr Fredrik Gjertsen had moved into a fashionable address in Oslo (then Christiania) in 1875. Further research identified that this person was Colonel Giert Gjertsen—Fredrik Gjertsen's elder brother. Colonel Gjertsen served as officer in the British Indian Police force from 1858 to 1882. (See below)

Colonel Gjertsen could have ordered the carpet from a number of carpet-producing areas in India at that time. The design, material, size, and execution, however, have considerable similarity with carpets produced around the same period in the nizam's workshop in Hyderabad. Identifying Hyderabad as its place of production is also supported by the information that most of Colonel Giertsen police career in India took place in what today is the northern part of the state of Karnataka—and in close proximity to Hyderabad.

The carpet was initially and through the latter part of the nineteenth century used in Fredrik Gjertsen's fashionable address in Oslo. After Gjertsen's demise in 1904, his daughter, Ms Louise (Gjertsen) Sommerfelt, inherited the carpet and moved it to Trondheim. When she died her husband, Mr Axel Sommerfelt remarried. In her late years, his new wife became somewhat eccentric and the carpet ended bundled up in the doghouse as a resting place for her pets. After her death in 1931 the carpet was rescued by Ms Smiseth's grandparents, Professor Alf and Aimee Sommerfelt, and placed in their library at Sandbakken. Here it had remained for more than sixty years.

Subsequent to my first visit to Sandbakken, the carpet was brought down from the attic, and my assumptions were generally confirmed. The carpet was large—about 19' x 16'—and most probably from Hyderabad in the Deccan plateau of India.

The carpet's story is also made interesting by the life of the individual who ordered the carpet; the person to whom it was given; those who inherited it; and those who by all likelihood tread on, and admired it.

The man who ordered the carpet was unquestionably a remarkable adventurer. Being born into a wealthy trading and shipping family on the south coast of Norway in 1825 he had the fortune of a good upbringing and education, and in 1844, he embarked on his medical studies at the University of Christiania.

The Sandbakken Library

Neither the capital of Norway, nor the medical studies seemed to have full-filled Gjertsen's adventurous disposition. Therefore, when the First Danish–German war broke out in 1848 he left his studies and volunteered for the Danish forces. The war was, however, short and following the ceasefire in August the same year Giert Gjertsen grabbed an offer to take an officers' course in Copenhagen. This he completed before returning to Norway in 1849 where he resumed his medical studies. Having obtaining his degree in the summer of 1853, he chose to work as a doctor among the victims of cholera epidemics—first in the town of Moss, and thereafter in Kristiansand. In mid-1900, this was a risky occupation as vaccines had yet to be developed.

While working in Kristiansand in 1854 he accepted a request to join a British troopship who as part of their involvement in the Crime War carried cholera-infected French soldiers from Oland to France. For yet again accepting such risk, he was when arriving in France awarded the Grand Medaille d'Honneur.

Thereafter he joined the British German Legions 2. Hussar Regiment as second lieutenant, but was quickly promoted to premier lieutenant. His regiment was, however, disbanded at end of 1856. After some six months in Paris, Gjertsen decided to seek his fortunes outside Europe. He therefore boarded a Norwegian freighter headed for Constantinople. From there the voyage continued into the Black Sea and ended in Trabzon. Trabzon was at that time an important harbour, being the most western entry of the Silk Route. December and November of 1857 found him on his way to Teheran on horseback. Here he spent a few months before he together with some British officers in May 1858 started on a journey through Isfahan, Persepolis, and Shiraz, on their way to the port town of Bandar-e Bushehr. From there a British warship took them to Bombay—their intended destination.

In Bombay Gjertsen accepted the post of deputy superintendent of police in the town of Belgaum. In this capacity, he in 1859 led a number of raids against remains of Indian soldiers who had participated in the First War of Independence of 1857. For his effort he was awarded the Mutiny Medal and was in 1863 promoted to chief superintendent in neighbouring Dharwar. In 1872, he was further promoted to district superintendent (with the rank of colonel) in the district of Tanna. Here he remained until he retired and went back to Norway in 1882. The carpet was brought with him and given to his brother. Apparently as a token of gratitude for taking care of his children while he and his wife were in India. A remarkable adventurer and an interesting carpet. Based on above one can safely date the carpet to somewhere between 1972 and 1981.

Of Fredrik Gjertsen, it is documented that he was an acknowledged scholar and educationist who in 1869 established one of the first private educational institutions preparing students for matriculation at the University of Christiania. In recognition of his contribution to furthering higher education in Norway. He was also a writer, poet, a bit of an activist, and a great speaker. He was in knighted the Royal order of St. Olav in 1888, and became a recognized member of the Christiania society. He entertained prominent people and the art elite of the time in his home in one of the fashionable addresses of the capital. This group would have included people like Bjørnstjerne Bjørnson, Henrik Ibsen, young Knut Hamsun, the Vigeland brothers, the painter Krogh, and possibly also Krogh's pupil at the time, Edvard Munch. All of whom are likely to have trod on this very carpet.

A similar honour befell the carpet during the ownership of Alf and Aimée Sommerfelt. She was as mentioned above a recognized Norwegian author of children literature, with books translated and printed in more than thirty languages. Professor Sommerfelt on his part is recognized as the most prominent Norwegian linguists of the twentieth century. He was one of the initiators and founders of UNESCO, and board member during its formative years. He is noted for his ability to build relations, to maintain an extensive Norwegian and international network, and for having used his own home, Sandbakken, and its library for academic and international discourses.

Smiseth Carpet prior to restoration
Probably Hyderabad 1875–80
580 x 525 cm (19'11" x 16") original

With such a history behind it, the family naturally wanted to get the carpet back to its former place, if possible. However, being very large it had not been possible to change its position to avoid the constant wear along typical walking pattern in the library. On this area, there was therefore hardly any pile left and the structure of the carpet was weak. Neither, did it help that it was a bit too wide for the library and therefore had to been folded. The rest of the structure was, however, sound and still had a good pile.

It became apparent that if the carpet should be of any use to the family an extensive renovation would be required, a renovation that likely would include removing the worst worn belt that ran straight across the breath of the carpet. Such action is of course generally not recommended. After having discussed the pros and cons the family, decided to explore this avenue since their interest was not in selling, but in bringing the carpet back to its rightful place for its continued admiration. I consequently entered into a discussion with my carpetwallah—Sayeed Ali—on the possibility of getting the carpet restored. After he had agreed to see what he could do, and provided an approximate estimate for such work. Thereafter the carpet was shipped to New Delhi courtesy the Scandinavian Airline System (SAS).

The outer border

After having studied the carpet, Sayeed Ali was certain that he would be able to carry out a satisfactory restoration. He was, however, not happy with the idea to reduce the carpet. In his view he could restore also the extensively damages areas and he would much rather buy the carpet as it was, and offered a substantial amount. For that amount he felt the owners could finance the purchase of another good carpet that fitted their requirements.

For the Smiseths selling the carpet was not an option, but neither could they have a carpet that would again end up being damaged. Sayeed Ali relented and went ahead with the help of a young expert weaver and a master dyer. The whole process, including that of searching for the appropriate material, took more than a year. However, in the end Ali kept through to his promise and returned a carpet where even trained eyes have found it difficult to detect the areas that have been renovated.

6
About Jail Carpets

In late 1992, I started noticing references to Indian jail carpets in carpet magazines. I also came across a citation of Ian Bennett about such carpets—a citation that later has been recognized as coming from Bennett's writing on an exhibition of nineteenth-century Indian carpets in London in 1987.[1] From this and the prices such carpets seemed to obtain at auction houses the interest was kindled. At about the same time an old copy of *Marg* surfaced entirely dedicated to Indian carpets. Here jail carpets were only given a short and negative paragraph.[2] From other contemporary Indian writings on Indian textiles one also gained an impression that these carpets were rather not talked about. This made the whole issue even more interesting and led to what one could only call a fascination. Consequent discussions with Sayeed followed. He was aware of the existence of these carpets, but was not aware of the growing interest. He was also quite certain that there had been no such production in the jails in Kashmir. He would, however, start looking for specimens from other jails. The result is that I ended up with several samples—to my utter satisfaction.

WHO INTRODUCED THE IDEA?

Initial descriptions of carpet producing areas tend to start with a historic narrative of when, where, and why production is assumed to have started. In the case of jail carpets this presents one of many challenges as no explicit documentation have as yet been identified. This is surprising since the colonial bureaucracy generally was quite proficient in documenting such matters, and a number of monographs have been commissioned by the bureaucracy on carpet production in their geographical areas. People like J. F. Watson, G. Watt, and T. Harris must have spent considerable time and effort on the jail products, and should have had access to information on their background, but none of them seems to have looked upon the issue of its initial establishment as worth mentioning. Over the last decade, however, new research indicated that the idea—rather than coming from jails controlled by British India which some early sources assumed—had its origin in the princely states. From there it was picked up by the colonial administration and introduced to jails in British India. David Black, in his writing on Indian dhurrie production in jails, informs that 'they began when enlightened rulers

---

[1] Ian Bennett, *Jail Birds: An Exhibition of 19th Century Indian Carpets*, Kennedy Carpets, 1987.
[2] Kamala Devi Chattopadhyaya in *Marg*, p. 7.

tried to relieve the monotony of prison life by introducing crafts in their jails. The idea spread to other states and was eventually adopted by British administrated jails.' Asha Rani Mathur writes that Maharaja Sawai Ram Singh II of Jaipur was among the first to introduce this activity as part of his prison reforms in the early 1850s.[3] It is further documented that the princely state of Mysore had sent a carpet produced in the Amherst jail to an exhibition as early as in 1857.[4]

From monographs, it is clear that many of the jails produced both piled carpets and dhurries. It is therefore fair to assume that jails in princely states such as Jaipur, Bikaner, Hyderabad, or Bangalore also would have made piled carpets from the time that production of floor coverings were introduced. It should also be noted that the official catalogue from the Colonial and Indian Exhibition at London in 1986 mentions that the jail production was 'introduced by the Government of India about twenty years ago'.[5] This would support the statement of Latimer that the jail production in Punjab had started before 1862 when the first batch of jail carpets were sent to the International Exhibition in London.[6] That the involvement in the princely states has not been picked up by the above mentioned gentlemen is, however, not completely surprising as none of them dealt with productions in the princely states in any detail. Or, the case might also be that none found it polite to bell the cat on an issue which—as described below—unquestionably had become quite contentious.

FOR WHAT PURPOSE WAS PRODUCTION STARTED IN BRITISH RULED INDIA?

It is likewise difficult to find documentation that clearly identifies the reason for introduction of carpet making into the penitentiary institutions of British India. The introduction in itself is peculiar since Tirthankar Roy has identified documents which dictated that only manufacturing catering for government demand were permitted in the jails.[7] Neither is it likely that it was introduced as a reaction to shortage of supply following the Great Exhibition of 1851 in London, as the introduction into the jails by all probability started ten years later.

By using the rather derogatory term 'Thug carpets' when referring to jail products, Birdwood indicates a potentially important connection between the need to gainfully occupy a large-scale influx of long-term prisoners that followed the British suppression of the Thugees and Pindaris in

---

[3]Steven Cohen, *The Unappreciated Dhurrie*; David Black, Oriental Carpets, 1982, p. 18; and Asha Rani Mathur, *Indian Carpets: A Hand-knotted Heritage*, Rupa & Co 2004, p. 72.
[4]Balfoure, *Madras Exhibition*, p. 149.
[5]Official Catalogue for the Colonial and Indian Exhibition London 1886, p. 18.
[6]Bennett, *Jail Birds*.
[7]Padmani Swaminathan, *Prison as Factory: A Study of Jail Manufactures in the Madras Presidency Studies in History*, New Series, 11, 1195.

central India. Roy was, however, unable to identify any direct proof supporting the notion that the first generation of jail-weavers was Thugees or Pindaris.

Another reason could possibly be that a considerable number of 'non-criminal' prisoners would have had to be accommodated in the years following the First War of Independence of 1857. It is documented that it was long-term convicts with an aptitude for weaving who were trained for pile carpet productions. Many of the prisoners from that event would have received long sentences. A large influx of this kind can have been a reason for changing the basic rules for jail manufacturing.[8]

Finally, it cannot be ruled out that the contribution this production made to the running of the penitentiaries was a significant contributing factor—even if this is mentioned as an added benefit, rather than the main reason for its initiation.

THE DEBATE ABOUT THE JAIL PRODUCTION

Documentation relating to the entire issue of carpetmaking as a commercial activity in the prisons indicates—in spite of the polite language of the exchanges—quite a heated debate that continued with some of the same contestants in participation throughout a period of some thirty years.

Sir George Birdwood claims that he already in 1878 lamented the jail carpet, their unfair competition, and cheapening effect on the Indian carpet production as a whole. His criticism of cheapening the production should, however, more appropriately have been directed at the commercialisation of carpetmaking in general, rather than the jail production specifically.[9] But the outburst might have had some effect. The official catalogue from the Colonial and Indian Exhibition in London in 1986 can, for instance, be interpreted as raising a concern over the fact that nearly all the carpets shown at this exhibition were jail products, and the basic criticism against the practice was reiterated. However, the catalogue also stressed that efforts were being made to improve the quality of this production.[10]

T. N. Mukharji—who in 1888 might have had opportunity of viewing more 'matured' products from jails—has a somewhat more balanced view. First, he recognizes that the days of the patronage culture of old is on the wane. Secondly, in referring to the copying of a Herati inspired carpet from the Jaipur collection at the Agra Central Prison, he recognizes the quality that a jail production can accomplish. He further points out as a mitigating circumstance the prohibitive cost production of

---

[8]Harris, *Monograph*, p. 18.
[9]Birdwood, *Industrial Arts of India*.
[10]Official Catalogue for the Colonial and Indian Exhibition, London 1886, p. 18.

such product would have in the context of the market place. This is demonstrated by describing the type of material that went into the carpet in question and that producing this carpet with 400 knots/square would require 40 minutes/ square inches as against only 6.5 minutes for a carpet of ordinary good quality. Finally, he recognizes that when being in competition with private firms the jail production had in some cases hurt the private entities. He also raised the question as to where entrepreneurs were to be found that would have the capital and the courage to venture such risks as an excellent production requires. He therefore concludes by proposing that the jails should continue their top-quality productions, but leave the mass production at the hands of the private manufacturers. In this manner, the jails could become the models of excellence that other producers could be measured by. He finally returns to the basics of fine carpet production in India—the patronage culture and states: 'the best works of art, which is impossible to produce in the ordinary course of trade competition, have always been encouraged, improved, and preserved by state interference.'[11]

In his book *Oriental Rugs* published in 1901, John Kimberly Mumford was also very critical of the jail production. In his opinion the spread of the jail production all over the subcontinent was the main cause of the deterioration experienced in the Indian carpet production in the late nineteenth century. Mumford bases his opinion on an assumption that 'it is almost inexplicable that a system so strongly grounded, so literally and figuratively interwoven with the family and civil life of the people, could, in so brief a time, have been destroyed, but such seems to have been the case'. Further that 'brought thus into competition with prison labour, the cast weaver was undersold, and had no resource save to cheapen his product and increase its volume'.[12] In this he undoubtedly took his clue from Birdwood but was more explicit in targeting his criticism.

Because of his extensive experiences with Turkish and Persian carpets Mumford was at the turn of the twentieth century a recognized American authority on carpets, and his writing had a significant circulation. This was likely the reason why Sir George Watt already in his introduction to the official catalogue of the Delhi Exhibition in 1903 found it necessary to oppose Mumford's views emphatically. Watts differed both on the basis for Mumford's views and his conclusion.

First, he convincingly argues against overstating the magnitude of the jail production by pointing out that by all likelihood the production in the private sector in Amritsar alone was larger than the entire jail industry put together. Secondly, he explains that carpetmaking in India was an art and

---
[11]Mukharji, Art-Manufactures of India, Glasgow Exhibition, 1888.
[12]Mumford, Oriental Rugs, 1901, p. 254.

craft imported by Muslims and supervised by Muslim rulers. The issue of caste therefore was of little consequence to the traditions of carpetmaking at that time, as indeed it was in the end of the nineteenth century. Finally, while recognizing the problems of the Indian carpet industry, he places the deterioration in quality squarely in the court of those who ordered carpets:

> But in fairness to those (in the Government) who have interested themselves in the modern traffic, it must be upheld, in the clearest possible manner, that the mistakes that have been made are entirely a consequence of the European and American dictation of supply. Oriental carpets are of necessity expensive and traffic in them must be restricted. The idea seems to have at once occurred that if cheaper articles could be produced by India than comes from Turkey and Persia, a large profitable trade might be organised. Patterns were accordingly sent to India, the quality prescribed, and the price fixed at almost impossible figure. The result could hardly have been otherwise than a steady deterioration in quality and artistic merit.[13]

In spite of Watt's arguments and that of others during the end of the nineteenth and beginning of the twentieth century, Mumford's views seem to have continued to be fielded as negative factors related to these products up to resent times, both in India and abroad. They are even in some cases used as background for criticism of Indian carpet production generally. The reason might be that Mulford's writing was in the form of an easily accessible publication while other writings on the subject as stated by Ian Bennett have been 'in a decidedly inaccessible form'.[14]

However, also Tirthankar Roy in a balanced presentation of his resent research acknowledge that the jail production at a general level subdued the private carpet industry. This was particularly the case where the private production was weak—as was the case in several of the carpet-producing localities in the southern part of the subcontinent.[15]

In addition to what is mentioned above, jail carpets were criticized for poor design, poor dyes, and poor material. These views seem to have been based on the assumption that few masters of the art would be convicts. One therefore inferred that the prisons only had access to inferior designers, dyers, or weavers. Since the weavers themselves normally would not have any tradition in carpetmaking the consequence would be poor designs.

---

[13] Watt, *Indian Art at Delhi*, 1903, pp. 426–27.
[14] Bennet, *Jail Birds*.
[15] Roy, *Traditional Industry in the Economy of Colonial India*, p. 207.

There are, however, clear indications that jails hired non-convicts as designers, dyers, and master weavers for training and supervising the convicts.[16] It is similarly documented that several of the jails had secured good patterns of Persian copies but also developed interesting new patterns. In addition, it was common that jails all over the country exchanged designs as well as patterns as well as designers, and thereby had the opportunity to gradually improve the quality of their production.[17] Finally, while there certainly are samples of these carpets still in existence that never should enter an exhibition, the majority cannot in any manner be regarded as a testament to poor or uninteresting designs, poor material or shoddy workmanship. This is clearly shown in the Jail Birds exhibition, and in those presented to the writer in Delhi during the period from 1996 to 2007.

In evaluating the experiment—an appropriate term for the seventy years of jail production on the subcontinent—it must also be taken into account documented evidence that jail production in some areas had a stimulating effect on the private sector production. Released convicts trained in carpetmaking are credited with the revival in Amritsar and Elluru carpet production in the latter part of the nineteenth century.[18] The production in Shahjahanpur were started by a released 'dacoit' trained in that area's prison.[19] In the revival of private carpet production in Agra, released prisoners provided important weaver capacity. Roy argues that the private sector that gradually took over the export industry in Amritsar also benefitted from the positive image the jail production had created.[20] Jaipur, which had very little of carpet production prior to the mid-nineteenth century today have a thriving industry—not the least thanks to the maharaja establishing the jail production.[21] The same can be argued in the case of Agra.[22] Mukharji and Watts emphasize the important role some of the prisons played in securing and conserving old designs by re-preparing and reproducing such designs that otherwise most likely would have been lost forever.[23]

Into this equation, one must also add that jails produced a significant number of carpets on special orders from colonial administrators, officers, local rulers, and wealthy merchants. By this, in a manner of speaking, the jails continued a patronage culture that at all times have proven a good environment

---

[16] Harris, *Monograph*, p. 18.
[17] Watt, *Indian Art at Delhi*; Harris: *Monograph*; Cohen, *Unappreciated Dhurrie*, Black, *Oriental Carpets*, p. 16; Bennett, *Jail Birds*.
[18] Roy, *Traditional Industry*, pp. 206–207.
[19] Dhamija, *Marg*, p. 29.
[20] Roy, *Traditional Industry*, p. 207.
[21] Watt, Indian Art at Delhi, pp. 434–35.
[22] Ibid., pp. 436–37.
[23] Mukharji, Art-Manufactures of India, p. 393; Watt: Indian Art at Delhi, p. 443.

for Indian carpet production—carpets that have merit both in terms of design and workmanship.[24] Such productions were running parallel with the 'commercial and export productions' but could never compete with these either in terms of price or timely delivery. They, however, did compete with good 'free' artisans who were unable to adjust to a time where the traditional patronage system no longer existed.[25]

THE EXTENT OF JAIL PRODUCTION

In spite of the criticism, carpet production spread quite rapidly to a large number of jails both in British India as well as in the princely states. Only by going through the more available material, the author has identified production in the jails as follows:

In the native states: Jaipur, Bikaner, Ajmer, Alwar, Patiala, Rampur, Kota, Nablia, Samatwadi, Shikarpur, Bahawalpu, Baroda, Hyderabad, Golconda, Warangal, and Gulbarg.

In 'old' Punjab: Delhi, Hassanpur in Gurgaon, Amritsar, Lahore, Montgomery.

In the north-west: Multan, Hissar, Dera Ismail Khan, Rawalpindi, Sialkot, and Peshawar.

In the west: Yerawada in Pune, Thane, Karachi, Cambay, Hyderabad, Gujarat, Ratnagiri, Ahmedabad, and Indore.

In the Ganges delta: Basti, Benares, Ambala, Jehlan, Allahabad, Agra, Lucknow, Bareilly, Fatehgarh, Kanpur, and Buxar.

In the South: Madras, Vellore, Tanjour, Rajamundry.

All told around fifty places of production. A considerable number of these are documented to be in existence already in 1888. Among these fifty the jails Yerawada, Hyderabad (state of Hyderabad), Vellore, Bangalore, Agra, Jaipur, Bikaner, Alwar, Ajmer are mentioned as having the better and/or larger productions.

Some of these jails had a considerable production. This was certainly the case with Agra, Yerawada, Bangalore, Lahore, Rajahmundry, and it is documented that Vellore jail employed 135 convicts on some thirty looms at the end of the century.[26] The rest were smaller units. Some concentrated on

---
[24]Cohen and Lucy Trench in *World Rugs & Carpets*, Country Life, 1982, p. 195.
[25]Roy, *Traditional Industry*, p. 210; Cohen, *Unappreciated Dhurrie*, Black, *Oriental Carpets*, p. 18.
[26]Roy, *Traditional Industry*, p. 207.

exports; others catered more to the local market. Most seem to have accommodated production on specific orders, and it is reported that in Bangalore jail, with sixty-two weavers, piled carpets were only made to order.[27]

According to Tirthankar Roy Amritsar jail too produced quality carpets. This leaves Kashmir being the only major carpet producing area without direct influence of jail productions. Kashmir was at this time an important state with a progressive ruler. It would be worth a study to identify the reason for a decision not to embark on a venture so many of his compatriots had chosen. Without such study one can only speculate. However, being a Hindu ruler in a majority Muslim state, and a state with a strong carpet making tradition which was practised exclusively by members of this majority, might be a compelling reason. This might also have been a reason why the Kashmir government banned import of aniline dyes as soon as its significant problems were recognized.[28]

As mentioned above production of piled carpets in the jails on the subcontinent initially seems to have started a few years after the mid-nineteenth century and reached its peak production in the early years of the twentieth century. Thereafter it went into a gradual decline. This decline might have had many reasons: a natural decline in the number of long-term prisoners after eradication of the thugee problem; that the private industry gradually took over the export market as was the case in Amritsar[29]; or because more and more prisoners were used for producing government forms and documents and thereby re-establishing the old rule that prison labour should not be used for activities that competed with the private sector. If the latter was a significant reason, Henry T. Harris's plea might have been heard. In 1907, he wrote, 'Far be it for me to wish that the convicts should be treated in the manner depicted in "Never too late to mend". But I do wish that the convicts, while kept usefully employed, should be employed only on such occupations as are above all suspicion of coming in conflict with the interests of honest folk, whose traditional cast occupation should be protected".

ATTRIBUTION TO SPECIFIC JAILS

When viewing some of the carpets presented in the period up to the eighteen eighties it is possible to detect influence from more indigenous patterns. This was probably the consequence of the jails utilizing designers and master weavers from the local region in setting up their productions. These differences seem to be most pronounced between southern and northern products.

[27]Harris, *Monograph*, p. 18.
[28]H. T. Harris: p. 10.
[29]Bennett, *Jail Birds*.

For commercial reasons all Indian weavers have had to change patterns quite frequently. It is more seldom that the traditional structures of an area have changed. With exception of the carpets produced by people of Tibetan origin all Indian weavers use the Senneh or asymmetrical knot, but with variations. H. K. Wattal described in 1965 five different manners in which this knot is applied in North India, each giving a characteristic feel and behaviour of the carpet.[30] The quality of the cotton yarn or the wool will also dictate how fine a carpet can be made. Such elements would make it possible to attribute carpets to regions and sub-regions and would likely have been reflected in earlier jail carpets. Even if it might have taken more time, these differences can gradually have vanished as a consequence of interactions between the jails. Such was the case when the nizam of Hyderabad in the latter part of the nineteenth century secured Kashmiri carpet artisans to his workshops at Golconda. This kind of 'interference' might not have made much of an impact in the private industry where traditions would be ingrained and supervisors and weavers had power to resist. In the jails, where weavers would have to follow orders, changes could be more rapidly implemented.

One must assume that the exchange of more local patterns, the use of imported patterns combined with imported 'experts' across regional boundaries, gradually lead to productions where it became difficult to ascribe a specific carpet to a given jail or even a region based on their patterns.

Literature shows that jail centres as in the private industry produced carpets of all sizes. There are, however, indications that some of the larger units, possibly because they could afford construction of large looms and outlay of more capital in the production, concentrated on large sizes. In attributing a given carpet one could therefore argue that the larger carpets could most probably have been made at a few of the larger centres. However, as evidence for a particular attribution, this too would be vague. One should therefore follow Bennet's advice on attribution of jail carpet when he states that 'such clues as we have are vague to the point of uselessness and attributions on the whole must be made with care'.

At the same time my humble experience is that in the case of those who are continuously seeking and evaluating carpets and has to make their living of their ability to make sensible judgments, such hunch often proves to be relevant—as is the case with the best of the carpetwallahs of New Delhi.

---

[30]H. K. Wattal; *Marg*, Vol. XVIII, September 1965 p. 40.

SOME CONCLUDING REMARKS

Whatever the reasons might be, the issue of jail production of piled carpets as a competitor to private production all but disappeared by World War I.[31] There are some indications that it might have continued in some of the princely states.[32] While no longer being any contender in the market, even today carpetmaking continues in a few jails in India and Pakistan. Bangalore and Bikaner central jails are examples of such in India, and Montgomery Central Jail, in Pakistan. Given the history of former production as shown above this production should be made a topic for serious research.

Fortunately, with the recent work of people like Ian Bennett and Tirthankar Roy a renewed interest has been kindled, and the style and structures of these carpets are now increasingly being woven into new productions. One can therefore hope that those jail carpets that still exist can be appreciated and secured as samples of decorative art on their own individual merit, rather than being frowned upon based on where and by who they were produced, and a somewhat less than accurate analyses.

---

[31] Tirthankar Roy: Traditional Industry in the Economy of Colonial India, p. 208.
[32] In the web page of the formally Montgomery Central Jail in Pakistan it is, however, interesting to note that the tradition still continues.

THE AGRA JAIL PRODUCTION

Piled carpet production started in Agra around 1580 when Emperor Akbar brought in Persian artisans into India and started a royal carpet workshop in his palace in the city that at that time was the capital of his empire.[33] Agra continued to be an important carpet centre throughout the heyday of the Mughal dynasty, and several of the known carpets from this significant period of carpet productions are ascribed to Agra.[34] In the latter part of the eighteenth century, however, Agra's significance diminished, and with this also its importance as a carpet centre. The best of designers and weavers were encouraged to move to better pastures with lesser royalties and new rulers that emerged in other parts of North India during this period[35]. By the beginning of the nineteenth century, Agra no longer seems to attract any attention for its carpets.

As with other centres in similar situations one must, however, assume that production at a limited scale would have taken place with local and foreign dignitaries being the principal customers. This, along with the lure of a famous name, and its proximity to other smaller carpet making centres in Uttar Pradesh at the time, might have been the reason for the German firm Otto Weyland & Company to select Agra as their departure point into carpet production for export in the second quarter of the nineteenth century. This company continued its production in Agra up to 1921 when it was bought by the East Indian Carpet Company.

Tirthankar Roy and others writers[36] indicate that a compelling reason for introducing carpet production into jails was the need for meaningful employment to the substantial inflow of long-term prisoners during this period. The increased inflow was a consequence of the 'war' against thuggies and pandaries—two strong groups of robbers and highwaymen operating in the central parts of India. If the need to offer some reasonable employment was the reason behind this experiment Agra certainly was centrally located in the troubled area and had an established infrastructure for production of carpets. The Central Jail in Agra would therefore have been a natural candidate for an early entrant in the jail carpet experiment.

---

[33] Dhamija: Marg, Volume XVIII September 1965, nr 4, p. 24.
[34] Walker, *Flowers Underfoot*, Indian Carpets of the Mughal Era, Thames and Hudson Ltd 1998.
[35] Roy: Traditional Industry in the Economy of Colonial India, Cambridge, 1999, p. 200.
[36] Birdwood 1901, Watt 1903.

Based on this assumption, it can for lack of more substantial evidence be surmised that production in the Agra jail would have started sometime in the late eighteen-fifties or early sixties. Further both Birdwood and Mukharji in their writing from the early part of the 1880s refer to this production as if it has been going on for some time.

The surviving carpets attributed to Agra jails, shows varied and artistic designs that are both copies of older designs and indigenous creations from this period. They are typically made of quality material, with an interesting range of colours, and knotted on a firm back with stout cotton warp and weft. This is certainly reflected in four of the five carpets represented in this book—the fifth is also by many attributed to Agra jail but do not have as pronounced structure as expected of this jail production.

In his writing on the Calcutta International Exhibition in 1884 Sir William Tyler praises the workmanship of the Agra Central Jail in reconstructing a late seventeenth century herati-inspired carpet from the maharaja of Jaipur's collection. Carpets from this jail were later entered at the exhibition in Glasgow, were they also received commendation. And at the significant exhibition in Delhi in 2003 carpets from the Central Jail in Agra were awarded gold medals.[37] There is therefore good reason to assume that this jail both had a potential for and turned-out carpets of good quality.

It should also be noted that there is no evidence that jail production in the Agra area crowded out private production. This, however, seemed to be the case in some southern carpet producing centres. Quite the contrary, it is for instance recorded that the German firm Otto Weyland & Company gradually employed a considerable number of released prisoners who were trained in carpet production. And the existence of quality production in the jail may—as suggested by Mukharji—contributed to retaining quality where it otherwise were likely to have deteriorated.

If, however, the interest of a buyer particularly relates to carpets from Agra jails a word of warning might be in its place. Agra jail carpets started becoming interesting collector items in the late 1980s and early 1990s. Whether the interest that developed was in jail carpets generally or specifically in carpets from Agra jails is not known. However, given the number of jails that are recorded as producing commendable carpets the author found it somewhat surprising that so many of the carpets were attributed to Agra jails. At closer examination one would identify design or structural elements that pointed in directions that could be as, if not more interesting than Agra Central Jail. The tendency among carpet sellers to attribute carpets to Agra has likely been the same as when the

---

[37]Sir George Watt: Official Catalogue for Delhi Exhibition 1903, p. 436.

name of Bukhara was used in the case of Central Asian production—good commercial sense. Given the treasures that might be found among production from the multitude of jails that were involved, the tendency to attribute good samples of jail production to only a few jails should be desisted. Each surviving carpet should be subjected to an unbiased identification process. For serious arts students in India, it could be a rewarding challenge to dig into the archives of individual Indian jails in which floor coverings were produced—both knotted and dhurries—as subject for their thesis. Only by such thorough search can one expect to unravel what Ian Bennet quite rightly calls 'a somewhat annoying paradox'—that one knows that considerable information exists, but has not as yet been able to subject it to closer scrutiny.

Prison Weavers – Karachi 1873

PALMETTES AND BIRDS FROM AGRA JAIL

Place of Production: Very likely Agra Central Jail
Period of production: Fourth quarter of the nineteenth century
Size: 264 cm x 180 cm (6'8" x 5'11")
Material: Very good wool on sturdy cotton warp and weft
Knots: Senneh knot 210/sq. inch

As mentioned earlier I was fortunate to be shown a significant number of jail carpets in Delhi during between 1997 and 2007. This particular carpet is in many ways typical of those that I with good reasons felt could be accepted as having been produced in the Agra Central Jail.

The carpet has quite a heavy base of sturdy cotton warp and two strands of weft—one thin and one more sturdy—on which good woollen treads are tied with senneh knots at around 120/sq. inch. It has a rather special colour combination which has been made even more interesting by an obvious abrash.

The colour combination makes it unlikely that it is an outright copy of an existing carpet. It is more likely that the designer has been under strong influence and inspiration from a Persian carpet of the Safavid period, or carpets from the Mughal period which had survived in India. It is well documented that the Agra jail secured itself an excellent base of designs, continued development of patterns based on such inspiration. The Agra jail also receive carpets on loan from the maharaja of Jaipur in order to copy, and thereby secure these treasures for the future. The presented carpet could quite likely stem from such a base.

When viewing a photography of an early seventeenth century herati floral carpet in the Ian Bennet edited *Rugs and Carpets of the World* there can be little doubt about the origins of this design. The Shah Abbas palmettes in the corners, the cloud bands, and the thin vine or twigs connecting the palmettes are all there. In addition, however, one finds that birds—most probably pheasants—play an important role in this carpet. This was apparently seldom the case with the herati originals. It is therefore likely that the direct inspiration was a carpet from the Mughal period when such

'Indianization' of patterns where part of a natural integration of this art into Indian society.

The birds and their positions on the carpet contributes to make this carpet livelier than its original as it elegantly forces one to view the carpet from the centre and out rather than from one of the sides and in. This design element would have been even more relevant on a larger carpet. This might indicate that the carpet providing the inspiration would have been larger and meant to serve in a palace. This carpet on the other hand would more likely have been made for the living room of a well-to-do civil servant or merchant. It should also be noted that a carpet with similar central motif but with different colour scheme and size, has been made in 1930 in Jaipur Central Jail.[38]

---

[38] E. Gans-Ruedin, *Indian Carpets*, Thames and Hudson 1984, p 269

A QASHQAI-INSPIRED CARPET, AGRA JAIL

Place of production: Very likely Agra Central Jail
Year of production: Late nineteenth, early twentieth century
Size: 223cm x 146 cm (7'4" x 4'10")
Material: Good wool on thin warp and normal weft
Knot: Senneh knots, 225/square inch

The Delhi carpetwallahs I had consulted unanimously identified it as an Agra Central Jail production. There are good reasons for this assumption. The carpet has what might be termed 'a rather heavy feel'. This is created by a solid base of cotton warp and two plies of cotton weft. In this case the warp threads are thinner than what one normally would associate with Agra jail carpets, but this is compensated by a tight weave which results in every second warp thread becoming close to 'depressed', and with a slightly longer pile than would normally have been used in other Indian carpets with such tight knotting.[39]

The design has clearly a base in tribal Qashqai weaving. However, it is difficult to ascertain whether a picture of a Qashqai carpet has been an inspiration in designing the carpet or there has been a carpet available from which this is a true copy. After a closer scrutiny the author tends to believe that the latter is the case. While the overall structure seeks the customary symmetry around the middle, a closer look at the details will reveal that no such symmetry seems to be sought in the details. Further, the colours used in the central motifs are not consistent. It would be quite unlikely that a professional designer of the time would have created such deviations from standard practice. One could therefore infer that if a designer has been used in providing graphs for this production, he has been forced to create a true copy. Another more uncommon possibility is that a weaver has made the carpet by directly copying the design of an original. The colour combinations used is, however, much closer to contemporary pieces from Agra than original Qashqai carpets.

In spite of or maybe as much because of its irregularities in the design, its somewhat strange colour combinations, and areas of abrash it comes across as a carpet that demands to be noticed, grows on the viewer, and would give character to any room in which it is made a centrepiece. This is most likely the reason why it has survived through more than a century of changing circumstances.

---

[39] E. Gans-Ruedin, *Indian Carpets*, Thames and Hudson 1984 p. 26.

LATTICE-INSPIRED, AGRA JAIL

Place of production: Very likely Agra Central Jail
Year of production: Early twentieth century
Size: 210 cm x 122cm (7' x 4')
Material: Good wool on a sturdy Jaipur back.
Knots: Senneh knots, 225/square inch.

This is a lovely designed and executed carpet coloured in vegetable dyes. The dominating lattice or trellis element surfaces in Indian decorative arts from the mid-sixteenth century. It was used in marble walls; ceilings; or woodcarvings in many of the monumental buildings from the seventeenth century. It also appears in carpets from the important Mughal period. Hence, it is not surprising that the element also surfaced in the jail production from the latter part of the twentieth century as jails often secured the right to copy or use carpets from the Mughal period as inspiration for their own. This has been noted by several authors in connection with the production in the Agra Central Jail.[40]

The lattice pattern was, however, not an exclusive domain of the jail production. As mentioned earlier Akbar introduced piled carpet weaving by bringing Persian carpet makers to his royal workshops in places like Lahore, Fatehpur Sikri, and Agra around 1580. Many years prior to this, however, a group of Persian families had arrived in Masulipatnam and settled with carpet production in Elloru in the southeast of the continent.[41] One of the traditional patterns these people are said to have brought with them was that of the lattice in various forms. This over time acquired the local name Reddy Khani and has continued to be produced in Elloru.[42] Gradually carpet production started taking place in other wool producing areas in the Deccan such as Warangal, Golconda, and Hyderabad. The exhibition 'Flowers Underfoot: Carpets of the Mughal Era' in 1997 showed a number of carpets from the seventeenth century with the lattice pattern accredited to the Deccan area.[43] However, the style of trellises; the structure of the carpet; and the border leads me to conclude that Agra is a safer choice for its place of production.

---

[40] Mukherji: Catalogue for the Glasgow Exhibition 1988, page 389, Sir G. Watt: Catalogue – Delhi Exhibition 1903 p. 434.
[41] H.T. Harris: Monograph Carpet weaving Industry of Southern India, 1908.
[42] Jasleen Dhamija: *Marg*, Vol. XVIII, September 1965.
[43] Walker, *Flowers Underfoot*.

THE JAIPUR CENTRAL JAIL PRODUCTION

While Jaipur city for the last 170 years has been well-known for its carpets, most of its reputation has been connected with the fabulous collection which belongs to the maharajas of Jaipur—less for its own production.

However, it is already before the mid-seventeenth century recorded that a workshop for silk and woollen carpets existed in Amber—the forerunner to Jaipur as capital of Jaipur state. This workshop might have been set up in order to produce carpets for the palace at Amber Fort. The carpets in the 'Jaipur Collection' which seem to be tailor-made for the durbar halls might well have been made in this workshop.[44] Since then and up to the mid-nineteenth century no reference to carpet production in Jaipur has been identified.

What we do know is that Maharaja Sawai Ram Singh, the ruler of Jaipur, revitalized the industry in 1856 when he introduced carpet production in his jails as part of an important jail reform.[45] We, however, also know that the maharaja lent carpets from his valuable collection to prisons in Agra and Lahore for reproduction as late as the end of the 1860s[46]. One can therefore assume that the jail production initially was concentrated on flat-woven dhurries but gradually included piled woollen and cotton carpets.

In the *Imperial Gazetteer* of 1886 this jail production of dhurries and piled carpets are being mentioned and commended. It is further documented that woollen carpets were sent from the same jail to the Glasgow Exhibition in 1888. Further Watts writes as follows about carpets from Jaipur Central Jail in the official catalogue of the Imperial Exhibition in Delhi in 1902: 'These are beautifully finished, of excellent wool and splendid colours.'[47] The quality of the production seems to have been maintained during the first decade of the twentieth century.[48]

And Lieutenant-Colonel Benn in his revised version of *Notes on Jaipur* published in 1915 informs that the jail in addition to piled carpets make dhurries and weave cloth. He states that 'the carpet

---

[44]Asha Rani Matur: Indian Carpets – A Hand-knotted Heritage, Rupa & Co. 2004.
[45]E. Gans-Ruedin: Indian Carpets, Thames and Hudson 1984, p. 269.
[46]Mukkerjee.
[47]Watt p. 434.
[48]*The Imperial Gazetteer of 1908*, Vol. 3, p. 401.

industry has obtained a high degree of excellence, and the carpets turned out here are much in demand both in India, in Europe and in America. Persian, Turkish and Central Asian designs are copied'. Interestingly he also mentions that Bikaner wool is largely used 'as this is the best obtainable'. He further states that pile carpets are also made of cotton, and that these are made in all kind of designs. Finally, he confirms that the cotton dhurries made in this jail are of excellent quality and design.[49]

As mentioned earlier, there are good reasons to argue that the maharajas' initiatives to introduce carpetmaking into the jails—contrary to the critical views Birdwood raised on the issue of jail production [50] actually laid the foundation for the revival and development of a private production in Jaipur in the beginning of the twentieth century. Whether it was because of changing political sentiments or due to increased private competition, or both, jail production of piled carpets in Jaipur seems to have ceased after Independence. It is, however interesting to note that the jails still turn out good quality dhurries. More importantly, there are indications that some of the old patterns are still available.

---

[49] H.L. Showers: Notes on Jaipur – 1909 Revised by R.A.E. Benn 1916.
[50] Sir George Birdwood: The Industrial Arts of India 1884.

A cotton carpet, Jaipur Central Jail
Late nineteenth or early twentieth century
210 x 146 cm (7'5" x 4'5")

LOOK WHAT THE CAT DRAGGED IN
A COTTON PILED CARPET FROM THE JAIPUR CENTRAL JAIL

Place of production: Very likely Jaipur Central Jail
Year of production: Early twentieth century
Size : 226 cm x 136 cm (7'5"x 4'5")
Material: Cotton on cotton warp and weft
Knots: Senneh knots 120/square inch and a Panalidar back

Saturday mornings and early afternoons tended to be one of the precious few times of the week one could expect a few undisturbed hours at European embassies in New Delhi during the early years of the twenty-first century. These were years when India demonstrated itself as one of the most important emerging powers of the world. The reason for these moments of peace was partly that local politicians and bureaucrats at least officially had Saturday off. More so because the bureaucrats at home tend to sleep late; go skiing, jogging; or were compelled to spend time with their families. They therefore had to desist from using their newfound communication gadgets to drum up answers from the embassies. Answers to questions they felt their politician might ask, come Monday morning.

It was therefore with a slightly exasperated look my wife responded when the guards announced a visitor, and shortly thereafter called up the stairs from the entrance: 'Come and look what the cat just dragged in.' The proverbial cat in this case proved to be Mr Sayeed—our carpetwallah—and the mouse the carpet in question. As the carpet neither had been dusted nor washed my wife's expression painted a realistic impression. After a thorough washing, however, the pleasing qualities of the different elements in its design came to light as seen in the photograph.

Even if less noticed or written about, production of piled cotton carpets was quite common in several commercial workshops, and certainly in the jails in the latter part of the nineteenth and early part of the twentieth centuries. Already in 1866, J. F. Watson in a report to the secretary of state for India wrote: 'The third kind (of carpets) is made of cotton, like the first, but instead of presenting the plain surface of the two, a short thickset pile of cotton is worked into it.' He thereafter proceeds with a further description of the production process and presents a plate with watercolour detail of a most astonishing cotton carpet.[51]

Also Mukharji[52] in 1888 and Watt[53] in 1903 refer to such carpets being produced in many jails all over the subcontinent. One must assume that also patterns for the cotton pile carpets were circulated around in different jails, making it very difficult to attribute a carpet to a specific jail.

The centre panel of this specimen carry considerable similarities with the Warangal carpet presented by Watson, and even more with another Warangal carpet now in the Salar Jung Museum that was produced about the same time as this carpet.[54] But neither of these includes the 'star' which is so prominent in this production, and which are common in dhurries from Rajasthan. Further, the borders are dominated by palmettes that decidedly belong to the North Indian tradition. These are important indication but by no means conclusive evidence. Nevertheless I would venture the opinion Jaipur Jail is the most likely place of production. It is also my opinion that these interesting productions should make a fascinating topic of research for any serious student of Indian art.

---

[51] J. F. Watson: Textile manufactures and the costumes of the people of India, 1866.
[52] Mukkerji: Art-Manufactures of India, Catalogue for the Glasgow Exhibition 1888, p. 398.
[53] Sir George Watt: Official Catalogue for Delhi Imperial Exhibition 1903, p. 447.
[54] Marg vol XVIII Sept 1965, Jasmin Dhamija, *Survey of Pile Carpet Industry*, p. 33.

A JAILBIRD'S DESIGN

Place of production: Probably Jaipur Central Jail
Year of production: Early twentieth century
Size: 223 cm x 146 cm (7'4" x 4'10")
Material: Good wool on stout cotton warp and two strands weft;
Knots: Senneh knots 168/square inch and Jaipur back

This is certainly an interesting carpet, and one that demonstrates the difficulties in attributing jail productions to any given jail—or for that matter any given area on the subcontinent. When Mr Sayeed presented this carpet, he was hesitant in attributing it to a particular area, but because of the colour combinations he felt that Agra Central Jail would be the most likely place of production. This view was shared by other carpetwallahs for the same reason.

As mentioned earlier, the jails partly copied, partly used old patterns in designing their own creations, and partly exchanged patterns with other jails. One can, therefore, with good reason, argue that the design by itself is a poor yardstick for attribution. However, jails are known to have used local designers and master weavers to train the inmates. One can therefore possibly infer that where a jail design resembles local commercial productions, attributing a carpet with such design to a jail in that locality can be justified.

In this case the author has not been able to identify similar patters among carpets attributed to the Agra area—from prisons or otherwise. And while the structure of the back seems to be of the panalidar back type or pronounced ribs running down the back of the carpet which was normally the case in Agra Central Jail production—the carpet does not otherwise have the 'feel' of an Agra jail. The feel is closer to what is found in productions from Amritsar. (This type of argument, however, is, of course, precisely the kind of clues which Bennett quite rightly states are 'vague to the point of uselessness' and as a consequence advise that attributions generally should be done with caution.)

Nevertheless, it is tempting to continue trying an attribution by drawing attention to the different elements of the design. The dominating central element might—in spite of a somewhat distorted form—have its inspiration from carpets in the Jaipur or Bijapur collection. The border, however, has much in common with old dhurries from Rajasthan. The same can be said about the manner in which the flowers are depicted. The turtle/crab form found in the centre of the four columns is also surprising as they tend to be used in the borders of Indian carpets.[55]

While not having any conclusive evidence the author will on basis of the above tend to feel that the carpet is a production from one of the jails in Rajasthan. Probably from Jaipur where it is documented that both piled carpets and dhurries were produced. It is also documented that even today there are instances where imaginative inmates are given opportunity to weave dhurries of their own design,[56] and this might also have been the case with piled carpets in the past. It therefore cannot be ruled out that this carpet has been made by such an individual.

---

[55] Henry T. Harris, *Carpet weaving Industry of Southern India*, 1908, plate 4.
[56] Shankar/Housego: *Bridal Durries of India*, Mapin Publishing Ltd., 1997, p. 51.

ABOUT BIKANER AND ITS CENTRAL JAIL PRODUCTION

Bikaner is today a district in the north-western part of the state of Rajasthan. This was also the capital and seat of power of the rulers of the State of Bikaner. In spite of its location, the city is in growing.

This state was founded in the 1488 by Maharaja Rao Bika, a Rathore Rajput and one of the sons of Rao Joda who was the ruler of the important state of Marwar at that time. After a row with his father, Rao Bika along with an entourage of soldiers and followers left Marwar, went west and further into the desert. Here he established his own a seat of power in what today is Bikaner.

The fortune of the state and their maharajas seems to have been quite varied and turbulent, with both internal as well as external wars. The state was, however, also at regular intervals blessed with wise and effective rulers. During these times, the state developed and prospered. Two such progressive rulers were certainly Dungar Singh (1872–1887) and his brother Ganga Singh (1888–1943). The list of development activities initiated by these two maharajas are long and covers education; health; livestock breeding; famine relief during draughts; building of large irrigation schemes as means of permanent solution to draught problems; and industrialization of the state. Developments also included introduction of modern judicial systems with independent judges; local democracy, annual budgets and fiscal control measures; establishing of a modern police force, and introduction of jail reforms. In spite of being able to institute such changes in a very conservative society a ruler like Maharaja Ganga Singh found time to serve with his regiment in World War I; was the only non-Anglo member of the Imperial War cabinet; represented India at the Imperial conference and the British empire at the Versailles Peace Conference. In spite of these roles in the British empire he was recognized as one that left no opportunity to press the claim for Indian self-rule.

As part of the prison reforms, new lines of work were introduced into the Bikaner prisons as an alternative to the traditionally menial and back-breaking hard labour. One such activity was production of piled woollen carpets and cotton durries. Of this the *Imperial Gazetteer* of 1885 remarks that 'Jail manufactures yield a net profit of about Rs. 20.000 a year, and consist of carpets (specially famous at the Central Jail) rugs, woollen shawls, blankets, etc.'

In the past as well as today the Bikaner area is well known for producing some of the very best wool in India, as stated among other by Watt in 1902: 'In fact Bikaner produces the best wool in India, and it is thus pre-eminently suited to become a great carpet weaving centre.' Moreover, of the products exhibited at the Delhi Exhibition in 1902 he comments 'Bikaner has through the enlightened action of His Highness the Maharaja attained a higher position of merit than has been reached by any of the modern centres of production. The Vienna patters have been closely followed, the dyes carefully supervised and the wool used of superior quality.'[57]

On a lighter note, 'a story goes that the Maharaja of Bikaner on a visit to India, asked his aid to buy him a choice carpet, only to find, when the costliest available was unrolled in front of him, that it had been woven in one of his own jails.'[58]

---

[57] Sir George Watt: p. 435.
[58] Asha Rani Mathur, *Indian Carpets – A Hand-Knotted Heritage*, Rupa&Co. 2000, p. 73.

A SPECIAL CREATION, BIKANER JAIL

Place of production: Bikaner Central Jail
Year of production: First quarter of the twentieth century
Size: 208 cm x 122 cm (6'10" x 4')
Material: Very good wool on stout cotton warp and weft
Knots: Senneh knots, 256/square inch

There are carpets, and there are *carpets*, and collectors should follow the rule of not selling or trading away a piece bought for seemingly good reason just because one is presented with another attractive and interesting piece one so much would like to acquire. Regrettably I also in this case forgot, and the carpet was traded off to balance another purchase.

It is a well-made carpet with very good wool; good structure; and good colours in interesting combinations, and bearing no resemblance to the traditional Persian designs. The border elements are simple but effective and the central piece is uncluttered. The dominating motifs of the central element can have a basis in Hindu culture—the dominant religion in Bikaner—and the colour combination certainly is commonly used in Hindu paintings. The blue and orange elements bear strong resemblance to the boteh, while the two black figures resembles those found in the Elluru carpets from South India. However, without an indepth discussion with artists from the area, one reverts back to the unquestionable truth: that in the case of jail carpets one cannot be sure that the design of a carpet originates from the same place as it is produced.

Whatever one gradually might be able to unravel of its background I in my amateur opinion this case lost a unique piece of non-Islamic Indian design from the first quarter of the twentieth century.

A KURDISH-INSPIRED BIKANER JAIL CARPET

Place of production: Bikaner Central Jail
Year of production: First quarter of the twentieth century
Size: 119 cm x 205 cm (3'11"x6'9")
Material: Good Bikaner wool on a stout cotton warp and weft
Knots: Senneh knots 121/square inch

As it has been made clear the makers of jail carpets often copied carpets whether the original was a Persian carpet; one from the South of India; or from the Jaipur or Bijapur collection. This has most likely been the case with the one presented here where the original can be traced to a Kurdish pattern from the latter part of the nineteenth century depicted in Andrew Middleton's book *Rugs and Carpets*. Middleton comments about these carpets: 'Many have sombre colouring and are not very popular. This one is enlivened by use of green in the borders.' My carpet obviously must have been inspired by the latter. The border is, however, completely different from the one presented by Middleton. Whether this is because its 'model' also had a different colour or this was adjusted by the designer of my carpet we will never know.

It is an intricate design and with exception of a strong dominating and quite bright reddish colours it lacks the boldness that is so characteristic of productions from Agra, Yerawada and other more famous jails. In spite of or because of this the carpet still is beautiful, well-made, and carries some of the same attraction as those coming from the Kurdish villages.

Field detail   Corner detail

BENGALURU AND ITS CARPET PRODUCTION

Bengaluru is today known all over the world as India's Silicon Valley. Within India, the city is also recognized as an important research centre. Prior to 1960, it was primarily known as the garrison of the Madras Sappers, and a sought-after retirement place for high-level civil and military personnel. With a cool and dry climate, and many interesting historic places in reasonable proximity it is an underrated city for tourism. The area covered by the megacity of Bengaluru has a thousand-year-old history as a place for settlements. In the early twelfth century, it was re-established by the Hoysala king. It got its modern shape under Kempe Gowda in the early sixteenth century. The Mughals overran the existing kingdom in the seventeenth century. They in turn 'leased' the area to the king of Mysore in 1689 and it remained under Mysore rule through Haidar Ali and his even more famous son Tipu Sultan. It ended up as an integrated part of the British Indian empire after Tipu Sultan was defeated and killed by the British forces in 1791. Nominally, however, it remained as a part of the state of Mysore. The above must be regarded—at least within India—as common knowledge.

What is less known was that Bengaluru during the early 1980s had already a large carpet export. Unsubstantiated information indicates that Haidar Ali (1722–1782) was the first to establish carpet production in the state of Mysore with weavers he got from Golconda, Bijapur, and North India.[59] This, however, does not seem to have left any significant legacy. Harris also mentions that weaver families from Elluru set up production in the early 1880s. This corresponds with Mukharji's claim that 'Bangalore in Mysore had a large trade in woollen carpets. The trade has fallen off since the weavers took to dying the wool with aniline dyes. What are known as the "Bangalore carpets" are a speciality of the place. They are reversible, having the same pattern on both sides, and are noted for their durability.'[60] Given the choice of wording, it is here unlikely that this refers to jail products.

However, in 1903 Sir George Watt mentions 'the jail in Bangalore has for many years been noted for the good quality carpets turned out especially during the term of its administration by Colonel P. H. Benson. In the Exhibition will be seen some excellent carpets from that jail.'[61]

---

[59] H.T. Harris, a Monograph on the Carpet Weaving Industry in Southern India, 1908, p. 5.
[60] N.T. Mukharji, *Art-Manufactures of India*, Glasgow Exhibition, 1888 p. 396
[61] Sir George Watt: p. 442.

In 1909, Dr P. S. Achyuta Rao collected information on the carpet production in the Bangalore jail on behalf of H.T. Harris. The jail at that time had sixty-two convicts active on nine quite large looms. He points out that these were not professional weavers, but long-term agriculturalists or traders that showed aptitude for the craft and had the required an 'amount of intelligence' were trained for the task. The jail only produced carpets on order. No carpets are made for 'warehouses' for outside sale. This might indicate that the jails by this time could have received instructions not to compete with the 'free' carpet producers that prevailed parallel with the jail production.

Depending on the clients' interest, the jail produced carpet in a range quality ranging from 8 to 16 knots /sq. inch. The jail bought wool from contractors but did their own spinning and dyeing. A master artisan who was not a convict trained and supervised the convicts. Giving an indication of the difference in labour input for varying qualities Dr Rao indicates that a weaver on an average needs more than two and a half time as long time to knot a carpet of the 256 knots/sq. inch variety as a posed to those of 64 knot/sq. inch variety.[62]

While little is known about present-day production in the Bangalore Central Jail is that the practice of including carpet making as part of the work itinerary of the inmates have been continued up to today—or has been revived. As in the past, given the right circumstances, Bangalore Jail obviously has the potential of creating pieces of art, as well as giving inmates a skill that can be practised when released from their incarceration.

---

[62]H.T. Harris, a Monograph on the Carpet Weaving Industry in Southern India, 1908, p. 18.

A SPECIAL BOTEH AND HERATI INSPIRATION, BANGALORE CENTRAL JAIL

Place of production: Most probably Bangalore Central Jail
Year of production: Late nineteenth or early twentieth century
Size: 233 cm x 120 cm (7'6" x 3'11")
Material: Good wool on cotton warp and weft;
Knots: Senneh knots = 225/square inch
Colour: Vegetable dyes

This carpet is unquestionably produced with the same inspiration as one depicted in H. T. Harris extensive monograph on the carpet industry in South India depicted in 1908.[63]

Harris comments of the specimen he has photographed 'the ground pattern is a form of the Birjand-Sehna-Herati variant of the well-known Feraghan pattern, with a quite uncommon stiffness and harshness. The border is also a stiffly drawn form of the 'cone of Flame', 'Crown Jewel' or 'River loop' device. Made in the Bangalore Central Jail.

There can be no doubt that these carpets originate from the same base. However, the carpet the undersigned were able to secure in 2005 seems to have a higher knot count than Harris's carpet and thus provides a more refined presentation of the design. This carpet, therefore, does not present the stiffness or harshness Harris attributes to 'his' carpet. Another contributing factor might be the peculiar colour combinations utilized. For natural reasons, Harris has not been able to present the carpet in colours so the comparison between the two has to rest as a hypothesis.

It is also interesting that Harris in describing the 'boteh' element mentions several interpretations. He further mentions that the chief interpreter of Shah Nasr-ed-Din's claim that 'the device represents the chief ornament of the old Iranian crown, during one of the earliest dynasties; that the jewel was a composite one, of pear shape, and wrought of so many stones that, viewed from different sides, displayed a great variety of colours.'

---

[63] H.T. Harris, a Monograph on the Carpet Weaving Industry in Southern India, 1908 plate 19.

Corner present carpet

Corner detail
Carpet presented by H.T. Harris 1902

Harris continuous to write: 'If this explanation be correct, it is easy to understand the depth of sentiments connected with it. It is not to be supposed that the shape was chosen for such perpetuity without some real symbolic or religious reason. Taking into consideration the deep devotion to fire and the sun of the ancient Persians, there is no room to believe otherwise than that this crown-jewel shape represents, in its first meaning, the flame which they worshipped, and which is reverently worshiped to this day by their prosperity here in India and in Southern Persia.' Sir Birdwood argues a similar theory. Both these learned men might be right as far as the original symbolism of the boteh is concerned.

However, this is an Indian carpet. It was designed by someone who did not have the above information. Therefore, he/she might have looked upon the symbol as representing a lotus bud and therefore launched a seed or, a flower, inside the boteh to strengthen this interpretation. Whatever meaning the boteh is supposed to carry, one must agree with H. T. Harris that the shape it is given in this carpet is quite uncommon.

Given that a carpet with an identical pattern from the same period is attributed to the Bangalore Central Jail, there are strong reasons to assume that such is also the case with this carpet. When presented the carpet was, however, identified as having been produced at the Agra Jail. This, in spite of the fact that the manner in which it is knotted resembles other carpets from South India rather than the North. A possible alternative could be that this carpet was made by released convicts or other weavers operating outside the jail. However, given 'migration of influence' on jail production, the attribution has to remain as a strong theory.

7
The Unappreciated Dhurrie

All carpets hitherto presented, are knotted and all but one is produced with woollen pile. There are, however, a number of other floor covers produced in India. The most common of these is the dhurrie.[1]

Descriptions of Indian carpets should not be regarded as complete without at least a rudimentary presentation of this commodity. It should, however, be noted that a dhurrie, as with a piled carpet, could be a useful, but plain piece of carpet, or a piece of decorative art. Let me then also start this small presentation by positing that there is no less reason to purchase a well-designed and executed handmade dhurrie, as it is to purchase a similar quality Indian handmade piled carpet.

Dhurrie is a carpet of flat-woven floor or ground cover, usually made of cotton unlike a piled carpet, which usually is made of knotted wool or wool and cotton. In the Indian context, both are carpets and are known to interchange with cotton, wool, and silk. Particularly in South India, the use of silk is popular. Dhurrie is also the name of a material used to make a 'farcies', a large dhurrie made for ground cover in wedding tents and congregation halls. Similarly, a saphsa is a Muslim prayer rug for individuals, while 'mira saphsa' is a big dhurrie with compartments made for a mosque.[2]

Dhurries come in many colours and patterns, varying from simple strips to elaborate depiction of plants, birds, animals, and humans, or sophisticated geometrical presentations. The closer you come to power and wealth, the more elaborate the patterns tends to become, though not necessarily more artistic, as shown in *Bridal Durries of India* by Ann Shankar and Jenny Housego.[3]

The prerequisites for making a dhurrie is cotton, the knowledge of how to spin, and to master the art of weaving. Researchers tends to agree that people in the Indus Valley already had those prerequisites around 3000 BCE. One would therefore assume they would also have invented such a useful item as a dhurrie. Unfortunately, there is no proof that they did. However, there are indications of dhurrie productions dates back to the second century BCW.[4] Further, in 1961

---
[1] David Black, *The Unappreciated Dhurrie*, 1982, p. 8.
[2] Ann Shankar & Jenny Housego, *Bridle Dhurrie of India* – 1997, pp. 22–23.
[3] Ibid., pp.38–39.
[4] Ibid., p. 34.

a researcher came upon a copper plate from Vijayanagaratham. On the plate is inscribed a list of commercial items, and among these also dhurries. The plate is dated 1382 CE.[5] However, the 'earliest extant pieces of dhurrie' is dated as late as seventeenth century.[6] The above are indications that dhurries are indigenous to India, but there are still those who raise questions. More research is required—research that also includes the southern parts of India.

Dhurries are spread all over India, and have a considerable versatility. The thickness varies from fine, to decidedly coarse, depending on need. Similarly, the size has varied from individual prayer mats to does in mosques and churches. Other uses are as wraps for beddings when sleeping on the floor, or underlay for the charpoy (the Indian string bed). Texts and miniature paintings from the sixteenth century and onwards, shows that dhurries was used as ground cover in big tent camps for rajas and maharajas on the move, or used in durbar halls and in inner rooms of their palaces. For such occasions it is known that dhurries as large as 5 x 80 feet were in use.[7] Such dhurries were also used during the durbars in Delhi in 1903. The mid-nineteenth century also saw an increasing interest for 'rom-dhurries' among palace owners, those with urbane mansions, and the growing urbane upper middle class, following the 1851 exhibition in London.

Some of the reasons why the dhurrie after at least 2,200 years still are relevant is unquestionably its versatility, usefulness, and ability to please its owners. However, the dhurrie also had its assistants.

One such group are the farmers, female and male, who in many areas of India kept weaving their ground or floor cover, underlay for their charpoys, or at times even get together for producing a farcie for their gurdwara. As mentioned, it is not known when weaving became part of the farming communities' tradition, but we know it continues in different sizes, patterns, and colours.[8]

A second 'group' and one that brought inn artisans through the 'patronage system' also kept the knowledge of high-level dhurrie production intact. These 'patrons' included rulers such as the nizam of Hyderabad, maharajas of Jaipur, Bikaner, Rampur, and the ruler of Baroda, along with some wealthy businessmen. Several encourage their knotting and weaving teams to work in the same workshop, which apparently earlier was uncommon.[9] This might have contributed to a change of ideas and successful experiments with more interesting patterns on dhurries. Dhurries with the right blue are beautiful, but when this was the only alternative, it will have stifled the interest in dhurries.

---

[5]David Black, *The Unappreciated Dhurrie*, 1982, p. 9.
[6]Ibid., p. 79.
[7]Asha Rani Matur: Indian Carpets, 2004 p. 79.
[8]Ann Shankar & Jenny Housego, Bridal Durries of India p. 23.
[9]Tirthankara Roy, *Traditional Industry In The Economy of Colonial India*, 1999, p. 198.

Some of patrons participated at national and international exhibitions and received commendations. Through this they will have improved the image of Indian carpets production at home and abroad. In today's world, it is not uncommon that we look upon philanthropists and patrons with scepticism and expect them to have dubious motives. In this case, it must be remembered that most of these individuals were rulers of their own domain, and as such expected to be patrons of the arts. In this context, it is interesting to note the following statement by Georg C. Birdwood from 1884.

> In the east, as we have seen, the princes and great nobles, and wealthy gentry, who are the chief patrons of these grand fabrics, collect together in their own houses and palaces all who earn a reputation for superiority in any Manufacture. These skilled artificers receive a fixed salary, and daily rations, and are so little hurried in their work that they have plenty of time to execute private orders also. The salaries are continued even when through age or accidents they are past work; and on their death, they pass to their sons, should they have become skilled in their father's art. Upon the completion of any extraordinary work is submitted to the patron, and some honour is conferred on the artist, and his salary is increased. It is under such conditions that the best artwork of the East has always been produced.[10]

Moreover, in 1999, Tirthankar Roy states:[11]

> Before the advent of exports, carpets were made in a context of patronage, for special uses and/or users. Patronage, by definition is an exchange between an implicit guaranty and notional security of tenure. Both attributes weaken in the market here for it might also in this case be appropriate to give praise where praise is due.

A third contributing factor to development of the dhurrie seems to have come with introduction of knotted and woven carpet production in Indian jails. This started around 1859–60 and gradually covered most larger jails. Jail production has been discussed in detail in an earlier chapter.) What is interesting in this context is that there are a number of miniature paintings showing dhurries as floor or ground covers, and all with a pattern of stripes—preferably blue and white. Nearly all reports from the exhibition in Delhi in 1851 and onward also describe dhurries in the same fashion. This, at the same time as the 'palace workshops' had started producing dhurries with more interesting patterns. Probably with the hope of increasing the income, the British Indian jails were encouraged to do the same. The encouragement must have worked as Sir Georg Watt in connection with the 1903 Delhi Exhibition points out that 'it would take many pages to give a satisfactory account off

---
[10]Georg C. M. Birdwood, *Industrial Art Of India*, 1884, p. 346.
[11]Roy, *Traditional Industry*, p. 197.

all the varied assortment of daries and shatranjis on view', and he followed up with naming some twenty jails or companies from where they originated. He concluded:

> It is one out of a large series of splendid dhurries and shatranji that the writer found in the Yeroda Jail. These wonderful cotton carpets are doubles well known to the residents in the western India, but until shown on the walls of the exhibition were quite unknown to the bulk of persons who interest themselves in Indian Art Manufactures. They give a lesson that might well be learned by the manufacturers of cotton carpets throughout India, namely that if they would abandon the blue and white forms of daris and shatranjis and produce richer and more varied designs such as those of Poona daris, larger market might be found in India for shatranjis than has as yet been a. There can be little doubt that a cotton carpet, if neatly and substantially woven would be more acceptable to inhabitants of tropical countries than a woollen one. [12]

The jail production continued actively up to World War I. Thereafter production dwindled to near nonexistence due to poor marketing and management, or reduced number of long-sentence convicts. During this period, from around 1860 to 1920 the system of carpet production in the jail was under constant criticism. This was not from a quality or human point of view, but because normal business was unable to compete on equal terms. Quality wise, from human point of, and artistically the pride was very satisfactory—as many of the remaining pieces shows. By 1920, commercial interests would have taken over products with assistance of ex-convicts, and the export market for carpets generally was good up to the end of 1935. For structural reasons and World War II both export and the local market slumped. However, a commodity like dhurries seldom dies out completely. Some forty years later, a few people with a tradition and knowledge met another person with vision, contacts, and some capital—and after a while, the dhurrie revived and is back in business.

I will take this opportunity to express admiration and gratitude to Shyam Ahuja who took the risk to revive the dhurrie yet again and to express the hope that those now will follow patrons of old and see the value of artists who can ensure that new dhurries not only are utilitarian, but also artistic.

The two following dhurries represent, in my opinion, excellent samples of jail productions. The first as innovative, the second as very well executed traditional "room" dhurries. The third fulfills my hopes that—both producers and customers can look upon and treat dhurries as pieces of genuine Indian decorative art.

---

[12] Sir George Watt, Official Catalogue – Delhi Exhibition 1903, pp. 4456–57.

Norwegian diplomat Ambassador Jon Westborg (retd) was born in Darjeeling, India, in 1946, but spent most parts of his childhood at different mission-stations in Assam, and at a boarding school in Shillong, then the capital of Assam. At the age of thirteen, he moved to Norway. Ambassador Westborg is an Overseas Citizen of India.

He began his professional career as a town planner in Norway after securing multiple degrees in engineering. In 1972, he began working in refugee rehabilitation work in Bangladesh, subsequently moving on to work in roles spanning project administrator to secretary general in various countries in South Asia and Africa, with NGOs, governments, and private sector organizations. After earning an MPhil from the Cranfield School of Management, UK, in 1990, he joined as Councillor and Representative of NORAD in India, Bhutan, and Nepal at the Royal Norwegian Embassy in New Delhi, and became its deputy director general in 1993. Three years later, he was appointed Norway's Ambassador to Sri Lanka and Maldives and was a central figure in the Norwegian facilitation of the Sri Lankan peace process and ceasefire. In 2003, he was appointed Ambassador to India and Bhutan; he returned to Norway after four years. Prior to his retirement in 2010, he served as Ambassador/Special Envoy to the South Asia region. He is a Knight Commander of the Royal Norwegian Order of Merit.

His fascination with carpets dates back to his childhood, but only became a real passion and a subject of study during his first posting in Delhi in 1990.

Made in the USA
Las Vegas, NV
10 February 2026

ed206637-a41d-4e65-84a6-1ab1816069c7R02